Finding the Place

Margaret Collett

Finding the Place

for David and Macca

Acknowledgements

This book was written as part of a Graduate Certificate in Creative Industries at Central Queensland University, and I am very grateful for the help and support given me by Professor Donna Brien. My special thanks to all members of the Gloucester River Writers, to Rosalie and Howard and to my wonderful friends Liz, Noela, Ann, Catherine and Irene.

Finding the Place
ISBN 978 1 74027 942 0
Copyright © text Margaret Collett 2015
Cover photo: Brenda Eldridge

First published 2015 by
GINNINDERRA PRESS
PO Box 3461 Port Adelaide SA 5015
www.ginninderrapress.com.au

Although the small town of Tillers Gap may seem out of the way, it is one reward for those who venture off the beaten track along the western foothills of the Blue Mountains. A visit to this secluded gem is well worthwhile. The Beladgery River still runs clear and clean beside an area of abandoned mines and waterholes called Deep Pools. However, the water in these pools is very cold and swimming is not advised, even during the summer months. The town's broad main street is flanked by several fine old buildings and this part of Tillers Gap has the feel of a bygone era. However, appearances can be deceptive. A coal mine has opened only a few kilometres from these quaint streets. Only time will tell if this small pocket of real Australia will become again the bustling centre it was in the heady days when gold prospectors came from far and wide. For the moment, come to Tillers Gap to find out for yourself how welcoming this town is and enjoy all it has to offer.

Mitch

The paint's peeling here on the veranda
where I lean against it
to light another smoke.
Dark tonight. No stars,
no moon yet.
The kids are in bed at last.
That Cameron's a real
little bugger. Lately, Suze can't handle him.
When she's tired, she loses it,
and tonight she gave him a great whack
across his backside.
I heard skin sting through his pjs,
and saw his eyes,
but no way was he going to bawl.
He's sure been mucking up,
but geez, what do you do?
As she's always saying,

'You're hardly ever here.
When you are you're sleeping.
How would you know what it's like
what with Cam giving me cheek
and Carly whingeing all day
'cause her teeth are coming through?'

She's right, is Suzy,
but I'm just tryin' to make some kind of life for us,
and the money's real good.
The roster's pretty tough, though.
Day shifts on top of night shifts.
They don't give a stuff about us, really.
But what's a bloke s'posed to do?

Didn't finish school.
Couldn't hack it.
But I'm strong,
and reckon I'm a good worker.

Suze is in the kitchen doing the ironing.
I tell her, 'Why bother?'
In fact, it's embarrassing, wearing ironed stuff.
But she won't have it.

'No bloke of mine's going out
looking like he slept in his daks.'

Trouble is, when she's cranky,
she takes it out on the furniture
as well as the kids.
There she is now,
thumping down so hard
that the ironing board
creaks in fright.
Reckon the veranda's the best place
for me right now.

Y'know,
I grew up in this house.
My dad built it.
When we were kids, Brian and me
would hang out here
'specially on those cold, wet days.
It was good,
'cause you were kind of outside –
and in.
Safe.

We'd race our remote-controlled cars from Radio Shack,
or even kick a ball around.
There's plenty of space.
When Mum and Dad used to fight,
it was the best place to wait it out.
The yelling and screeching was muffled,
and you could look beyond,
out into the street,
where other people
had other lives.
You could stay until things settled again.
But those times,
it seemed like
there was room for only one of us out here.
Whoever got there first was the lucky one –
or the most desperate.
The other one was stuck in the bedroom.
When that was me,
I'd crawl head first down,
down,
under the blankets
to block out the racket.
Don't want that happening
to our kids.
So best if I stick out here,
until from inside comes the weary, grateful groan
of the ironing board as it collapses.

At night
you can see the glow from the mine.
They work it twenty-four/seven,
day and night.

I'm part of that.
It's okay, mostly. They're not bad,
the bunch of blokes I work with,
some are even mates.
You can get bloody tired and dirty.
It's usually a good kind of dirt,
honest dirt.
But tonight I feel a different
kind of grubby.
I've seen something at work
that I shouldn't've.
Something not right,
but can't unsee it.
Wish I could.
Worries me,
'cause it doesn't sit easy,
not with me, anyway.
But what to do?
Don't know, but it's eatin' at me
as I lean here,
the timber rough against my arm,
cigarette glowing
like the light from a tiny mine.

It was last night.
I was just coming off my shift.
Couldn't wait to take a leak
and went over to the edge
of the compound where the washery is.
The ground was still muddy
from all the rain lately.

I noticed that the dam holding the waste water
wasn't just bulging,
but overflowing,
the water making runnels
down the incline
onto the damp soil around it.
I stood there, gripping
the cyclone wire like a monkey at the zoo.
It was all quiet around me
except for this trickling sound
which meant
that waste was running off,
getting away from the holding pond.
I know some has come
over the lip of the pond before,
but not enough to flow like this.

I was about to go
and find someone to tell
when a guy came out from a shed.

'Hey, what you doing there, mate?' he called.
'Shouldn't you be goin' off shift?'

I explained that I needed a slash
and started to tell him about the overflow,
but he cut me short.

'Not your worry, mate.
Not your business.
You just stick
to what you know, eh.
Leave this to the big boys.'

Now I'm not a bloke
to get cranky quick,
but I didn't like the way he was talking to me.
After all, I work there too
and he was dressed just like me,
so he couldn't have been a big wig.
I went ahead and finished
what I was tryin' to say.
'You know that pond's overflowin',
don't you? There's river flats not far
from here, and with all that rain…'

But before I could finish,
his face was there,
pressed against the fence,
so that the wire
practically dug into his cheeks,
and I could see black stubble.

'Now, you look here, mate –'
and this time his 'mate' wasn't friendly –
'Just go home to the missus
and let us do our job.
Go on, beat it.'

He glared at my ID.
I wasn't exactly scared,
well, yes I was, a bit.
He called after me,
'And you'd better forget
what you just seen –
if you know what's good for you.'

But of course I can't forget.
And there was something
real sneaky about it all.
I know a lot of people
who think mining's gonna ruin the country.
I don't agree.
What's good for jobs
has got to be good for the area.
Just the same, I like where I live
and want my kids to grow up here.
If that stuff – and I've seen it in daylight –
gets into the river near town,
it's not good. That bloke
really got to me, really riled me,
tellin' me what I could and couldn't do.
I dunno. You don't just let
that sort of thing lie, do you?
Who can I tell, but?
Can't think of anyone who'd know what to do
or keep his mouth shut
until he'd worked somethin' out.
Maybe that minister across the road,
maybe he'd listen. They're s'posed
to be good at that.
They're not allowed to blab what they know, either.
So he might be a goer.
I'll see.

Ingrid

As soon as I turn off the highway
there's that feeling
of being closed in.
The scruffy trees that guard both sides of the track
lean over
and throw late afternoon shadows
that 'flack, flack'
across the windscreen
like an old sixteen-millimetre film unravelling.
There's the scent of leaves and damp soil
as the plants from Sydney
shuffle uncomfortably
on the car floor behind me.
They too seem restless,
reluctant travellers.
Last night's storm has brought down small branches
and there are still puddles
glinting in the potholes,
and 'miles to go before I sleep'.
This last part of returning to –
I can't bring myself to call it home –
is the hardest.
I feel somehow 'thinned out',
bored by a battle of my own making.

Instead of looking forward,
I find myself checking the rear-vision mirror,
almost expecting, hoping for
a police car, a friend, a chariot,
anything,
to come from behind, overtake

and block my path.
'You're going the wrong way,'
they'll say, and escort me back to the city.

That's when it happens.
I sense the car graze,
bump against something –
a wallaby, a fox
or maybe a fallen branch.
In the deepening gloom
I don't see it as much as feel it
just nudge the wheel,
but it's enough –
and the car skids on the slick surface
over to the wrong side.
There's soft soil and a tree.
Of course there's a tree.
This one maintains its position,
smack bang in the middle of my bumper bar.
I'm not going anywhere.
Not forward.
Not back.

I sit there for a minute or two.
Quite calm,
listening to the forest shifting, discussing
whether to make room for me
if I decide to venture further.
I don't feel sore,
not even a hint of whiplash.
But a heaviness settles somewhere in my shoulders,

and for a moment
I can't even be bothered to undo my seat belt.
I try my mobile,
but of course there's no signal.
Not in this god-forsaken place.
The car re-starts first go,
but when I try to reverse
there's a whining slush
that means the wheels are spinning in mud.
That's all I need.

Now it's starting to get 'proper dark'
as my sister would say when we were little.
I don't like it one bit.
Too damn quiet,
a waiting kind of quiet.
Thank God my torch is working.

'Always have a torch with you,'
says Clive.
And of course, he's right.
He's always right.

It's not long before there's the drone of a car,
then headlights
boring through the gloom.
It's going the same way I am –
or should have been.
I don't know whether
to be relieved or scared.
Could be an axe murderer.
Could be a carload of them.

Still, I feel both stupid and grateful
when the car slows,
pulls to the side of the road,
and stops.
I make out two men.
Two axe-murderers?
The driver leans over
and speaks to the other one,
who's bearded
and wearing an orange hi-vis shirt.
And then he gets out and comes over.
I realise it's the minister,
clergy-person, whatever.
He gave the talk at the ANZAC ceremony.

'Hi,' he says, as if we'd planned
to meet here all along.
'Tom Shelley.
Got a bit of a problem?'
His voice is deep and assured,
good for spruiking from the pulpit, I bet.

'You could say that.'
I try to sound as casual.
Don't want to explain to this God-botherer
why my car is kissing a tree
on the wrong side of the road.
But he doesn't ask.
Just says, 'You okay?'
and looks at me intently
as if hoping I'll confess
to something more interesting than tree-bashing.

All I'm prepared to give him
is 'I'm fine. Thank you.'

'Well, let's see what's what,' he says,
and goes to the front of the car.
'You know, there's not much wrong.
If we could just get this baby back onto the road.'
He pauses, smiles and says,
'Nice car, the Astra,'
giving the wheel a friendly kick.
'It's really just the soft ground.'
He pulls off his jumper
and passes it to me
as if I was his second in a duel.

Without thinking,
I put it around my shoulders.
It's still warm from his body.

'Why don't you hop in and start her and
we'll see what's what?'
I'm already irritated by his 'what's whats',
but do as I'm told.
The car starts fine first go,
but the front driver's wheel still spins.

'Right,' he says. 'A couple of branches should do.
Give us a bit of light,
and I'll grab what we need in a jiffy.'
A jiffy? What sort of man says 'jiffy'?

My torchlight follows him into the trees
where he bends and lifts some fully leaved branches
chucked there by yesterday's storm.
It's only then
I remember
the other man.
Is he still waiting with the axe?
Why just sit there?
What sort of useless specimen
leaves another bloke to do all the dirty work?
But when Mr Minister comes back
with his armload of small branches
and bends down to the offending wheel,
something stops me from asking.
A bit of male grunting,
and then he stands and gives me
a disarmingly boyish grin.

'Let's give it another go.'

This time, after a bit of whingeing,
the wheel seems to understand
there's something to latch onto
and I'm able to reverse the car onto the track.
It's now that I feel stupid,
facing the wrong direction.
But Preacher Man makes no comment.
He leans down to my window.
I can smell his faint sweat.

'You should be fine now.
I think we're going the same way,
aren't we?' – And even in the gloom
there's a hint of laughter
in his words.

'Yes. Yes, we are. I mean I am.
Thanks so much.'

'A pleasure, madam. Glad to be of service.'
And he doffs an imaginary cap.
That grin again.
'We'll follow you to town,
just to make sure.
Give us a jiffy and we're all set.'
With that, he sprints back to his car, starts it up,
and waits for me
to pull ahead of him.
All the way back,
I'm conscious of a pair of bright and steady lights
observing me from behind,
pushing me home.
I still have his jumper
across my shoulders
like a casual embrace.

Clive

Ingrid said she'd be home before dark
I waited until ten minutes
after official sunset time before I called.
But no signal on her mobile.
Nothing.
No beeps.
Not even the buzz
that says she's otherwise
engaged.
Just silence
and the text 'No signal.'
Much like things have been
between us lately.
I thought life here
would be a new start for us both,
a tree change, as they say.
But it's not that simple.
She misses the city and her friends.
I have my work,
as she often reminds me,
and was busy finishing the Bartlett account
so I did nothing.

Now I can hear her car.
I part the curtains, peering through
the gathering fog,
and she's getting out.
There's another car right behind hers
a four-wheel drive, dark colour.
The passenger's Mitch Larsen.
He works at the mine.

His wife cleans my office
and the house.
Ingrid walks around to speak to the driver,
but whoever it is,
pulls out, waves
and gives a quick beep of the horn.
What is going on here?
I'm still standing there,
thick curtain fabric between my fingers
when she opens the front door.
She doesn't put down her bags.

'Hello, Clive,' she says.
'How've you been?'
Doesn't look straight at me, but then
she rarely does these days.
'I'm exhausted.
Going to have a bath.
You'd better get yourself something to eat.
Don't know what I want.'

I'm still standing in the hallway,
with that wretched cat
wreathing itself around my legs,
leaving hair all over my trousers.
Ingrid's already running the bath.
I can hear the water
rumbling into the tub.
She'll be swirling in
some scented salts.
Steam will be filling the room.

She'll be undressing,
dropping underwear, her clothes
all over the tiles.
Her long, heavy hair
already damp as she twists it
up into a knot.

Here I stand
lost,
like a foreigner
in my own home.
What will I get for dinner?
I thought she'd be earlier
and would have had time to prepare it.
Have to make myself a sandwich
There's the ice cream I bought today.
Crème brûlée.
Ingrid's favourite.
That'll have to do.

The water's stopped running now,
and there's quiet –
except for Claudia the cat,
yowling for her food.
I suppose I'll have to get that too.
Ingrid will be lying there,
eyes closed,
her breasts breaking the water
soft breasts, hard nipples,
steam rising around her
like incense.

Time was, I'd just go and open the door
to her slow, lazy smile.
Bend to my knees and
silently lather her body.
But now I know not to.
The door's not locked,
but it might as well be.
She'll be lifting the flannel
from the water,
which she lets trickle onto her stomach.
I'd better eat
before she reappears.
I wish she'd call for a dry towel,
But she has everything she needs.
I'm hollow.
Knock me and I might break.
I reach for the loaf of bread.

Ingrid

I just had to get into the bath.
I can't deal with Clive right now.
He's so very…Clive.
I know he can't help it.
I only have baths
when I'm really cold
or need to think.
Like now.

During the night I dream.
Terrifying dreams
in gorgeous colours.
They say never to bore others by recounting your dreams,
so suffice to say in this one I was driving.
Couldn't see
where I was going
and for some reason
I was trying to steer from the back seat.
The windscreen was covered
in bird droppings
and I stopped to wipe them off
with a blue woollen jumper.

When I woke,
I was drained, aching,
as if I really had been driving all night.
Clive was snoring quietly beside me.
Even his snoring
is muted and restrained,
his pyjamas done right up
to the second top button.

The last things he does
before getting into bed?
Combs his hair and pulls down his pyjama top,
straight and neat.
He'd made no attempt at conversation.
Just read,
or pretended to,
until I must have gone to sleep.

I sometimes wish things were different
between us,
but at the moment,
don't have the strength
to do anything about it.
I don't know that the effort
would be worth it.
Still, I must try to be more attentive,
affectionate, accepting.
He's a good man,
and he's not the one
who's changed.
So why do I find him
so boring and irritating?

What should I do
with that pullover?
It's beautifully hand-knitted.
No idea where Preacher Man lives.
Maybe they put ministers right next to the church
so that they can nip over
and have a quick word with the Almighty
at a moment's notice.

In fact,
I don't even know which church he's in charge of.
I know where the Catholics are.
They always grab the highest point in a town,
or so my friend Theresa says.
Should I wash the jumper?
It's not dirty,
and I only had it around my shoulders
for a while.
Maybe his wife
is giving him the third degree about it already.
I'd better do something.
I feel guilty still having it,
close by
in my bedroom.

Zoe

The Careers teacher, Mrs Gauci,
warned me it would be like this:
sweeping the floor,
making cups of tea,
washing stuff, cleaning the mirrors.

'You'll be sorry you chose hairdressing
for work experience, Zoe.
It'll be just like housework.'

But I'm not sorry.
I like it here.
I'm not so stupid
to think they'd let me do Mrs McEwan's perm
or colour Jess Finlay's hair.
I'm only fifteen.
But there's a great feel to the place,
the smells – sort of antiseptic –
the foaming shampoo and hair colour,
the snick snick of scissors, hair sliding from
plastic capes to the floor.
There's always something going on,
and lots of laughter and gossip.
It's true what they say
about hairdressers
getting told everyone's secrets.
Found out today that the lady having the perm
has got Parkinson's disease,
whatever that is,
and Dave Keegan's been made redundant
from the mine.
I know that word.

Redundant.
Means you don't have a job
because they don't need you any more.
The man getting a number three says
his piles are giving him gyp.
Too much information.
Rhonda's a great cutter and a really nice lady too.
If there aren't any clients, she talks to me
about what hairdressing's really like, or
we look at the hairstyle books.
She's promised to put a stud in my chin.
Mum will probably charge down here
and chuck a hissy,
but it'll be too late by then.
Rhonda's got a small tatt
of the yin and yang symbol on her shoulder
but she keeps it covered.
She reckons some of the clients
would get put off by it.
I think it's cool.
Wish I had one.
The magazines in here are really daggy and old –
a bit like some of the clients.
(Rhonda says I have to call them clients
even though I know most of them.)
One *Woman's Day* is really floppy and worn
and even has stuff in it about Michael Jackson.

'Keep yourself busy and show some initiative.
Don't wait to be told what to do.'
Mrs Gauci again.

Bet she thinks
that because I want to be a hairdresser
the word 'initiative' is beyond me.
It's not, and I can even spell it.
I'll show them.
It's better here
than sitting in stupid lessons
and better here
than being at boring old home.
I get time off for lunch
and meet up with some of the others
also on work experience.
Anna's at the travel place,
Bree's doing 'retail',
which means she's at the supermarket,
and Nic's at the vet.

I really like Nic.
Liked him for a while now.
He doesn't do anything special.
but sometimes
I catch him
looking at me in that way
and think he likes me too.
He's got gorgeous brown eyes and dark hair.
My mum saw me walking to the park
with him and Bree yesterday.

She said, 'I don't want you
hanging around with that boy.
Hairdressing's bad enough,
but that has to stop.'

'Why?' I asked, though
I already knew the answer.
'Anyway, having lunch with friends isn't "hanging around".'
I love to get her going sometimes.
It's good fun.
Her eyes go all poppy
and she gets that cat's bum mouth.

'Don't contradict me, Zoe.
You know very well why.'

But she won't say it.
Won't admit it's because
Nic's mum is Aboriginal.
Don't know why she goes on about it so much.
No one cares these days.
Anyway, she went to school with Nic's dad.
Sometimes
she's such an old fart.
At lunch today Nic sat real close to me
and his arm brushed against mine.
He didn't move it,
just held it there,
so we sat together on the park bench.
Gave me goosebumps.
Nice ones.
Then he walked back with me to Rhonda's.
The long way round.
When we said 'See ya' and he walked away
I waited to see if he turned round.
And he did!
Can't wait till tomorrow!

When I was putting my overall back on
Rhonda said, 'Wasn't that Nic Salter just then?
Nice boy.
Seems to like you, Zoe.'

If other people notice, it must be true!
It made me go all funny inside.
One day I'll have my own salon.
I like that word 'salon'.
Sounds posh.
I'll call it 'Hair we are'.
Maybe Nic will be the vet by then,
and we can still meet for lunch.
That would be sooo cool!

Tom

On Tuesday I heard the mail bike
and came outside.
Could have sworn
that woman gave my letters the once-over
before handing them to me.
She won't find anything interesting there.
The bloke from across the road
called out and came over.
Just to say g'day, he said.
He seemed nervous, but that often happens.
People think I'm going to start bashing the Bible
or speaking in tongues.
Not my style, but guess he's not to know that.
We chatted for a while.

His name's Mitch Larsen.
He's got two young kids,
his wife's called Suzy
and he works at the mine.
Now that's something
I am likely to get a bit worked up about.
Not keen on what's happening to this area.
Haven't said much, just listened so far.
I'm seen as one of the 'blow-ins'
whose opinions don't count,
but it seems to me
that greed is eating up this beautiful valley.
But I didn't say that to my new friend.
Not the time.
Not the place.

Mitch asked if I drank.
I love that. They're wary, these people.
Sounds as though they're asking
if I'm an alcoholic.
I told him yes,
I enjoyed a beer, and he smiled.
Then he said would I like to go to the pub sometime.
I was chuffed, actually.
That's the first time anyone's asked
me out for a drink.
He suggested a pub a couple of villages away.
Surprised me, but what the heck.
So Thursday it was.
I offered to drive so that his wife could have the car
and, to be honest,
I thought he looked like the type
who could put a few away.
He seemed a bit unsettled,
edgy.
That Preacher Effect again.

It's 2 a.m. by the bedside clock.
Sunday morning.
I've always liked Sunday mornings.
There's a clean slate feel that's encouraging.
Two years yesterday
since Jen died –
late on Saturday night.
As if she didn't want to spoil Sunday for me.
She had tried to hang on,
but her injuries were too severe
and in the end,

even Jen couldn't win.
They didn't rush Rosie to hospital.
She'd gone before anyone could help.
I need to think she didn't hurt
too much.
I'd always tried to protect her from pain of any kind.
And here she was,
dying without me being there.
My whole body clenches
when I think about it.
All thirteen years of her,
leggy beauty that she was.
Tossing that long gold hair,
on the cusp of something wonderful, reaching out for life,
loving us and every minute of it.

But we'd argued
that morning.
She was doing her homework at the breakfast table,
smudging a map of some underdeveloped country
with sugary Weet-Bix.
I pointed out that
there were enough mountainous areas
in that region
without adding her three-dimensional ones.

'You should have finished that last night, sweetheart.'

'I would've,
if you hadn't made me go to bed so early.
Jesus, Dad, none of my friends
have to go to bed before nine.'

And it was her using that one word –
'Jesus' – that got me.
So what did I do?
I got angry.
'There's no need for that word,'
I said, my minister's voice
sharp and unyielding.
'You disappoint me, Rosie.'
My trump card.
Got her every time.
The tears welled
and one big one
plopped onto the map
of the already ravaged landscape.
But instead of being her loving father,
I pushed my point home as I would in a sermon.
'That's one thing I won't tolerate.
You know that.'

The books were closed,
shutting in maps, scraps of Weet-Bix
and tears.
She huddled her way out to the car
to wait for her mother.
Last words.

How can I live with this ache?
Tell me, how?
When I'm back in that morning,
it feels as though I'm being wrung out
like my mother would twist wet towels,
strangling water from them.

I can tell no one,
share with no one.
Just then, Jen came rushing out,
expertly scooping up her keys
from the disorder of the kitchen bench.
I was cheek-pecked,
shoulder-patted.

'Sorry, Tom. Late again.
Bye. Love you.'

I stood at the window,
breathing in a waft of Je Reviens.
They settled themselves
in the car.
Rosie's head lowered
as her mother spoke to her,
all the while twisting up
that bright red hair
using the rear-vision mirror.
Neither of them saw me wave
goodbye.

There's a quiet rage to grief,
an anger that we tamp down.
Most of the time it's a comfort,
knowing I've been so loved,
but sometimes
the pain narrows my throat
until I can barely utter a sound.
That's one reason I came to Tillers Gap.
Different state,
newish life.

Jen had never been here.
Saw an ad in the church paper for a minister.
They have to advertise now.
When I checked out the town on the internet,
I liked the look of it.
Don't think I had any competition for the placement.
They didn't say,
and I didn't ask.
They know I'm alone,
but I didn't even have to give too many details.

I love my flock.
They're mostly the older, faithful types.
Some, I think, have forgotten
why they come to church,
but still don't like me changing things.
Like Mr Emmerton, for instance,
with his little wife
trailing behind him,
casting apologetic looks my way.

'Not keen on that guitar of yours, young man.
Not in the Lord's house.'
That tells you something, him calling me
'young man'. I'm forty-six in July.
But I saw Mrs E
tapping her feet while I was playing!

Mrs Beattie has told me,
'I think people would take you more seriously
if you wore a coat and tie, Tom.'
Mr Wheeler actually walked out last week.

Must have been the mention
of asylum seekers.
Made a great show of it, too.

'Bah humbug, I say!'
Actually, I take it as a compliment when he does that.
I'm hitting home.
Or hitting something.
Jen would be proud of me.
But they're a good lot, really.
Just wish they'd stop with the casseroles!
There's warmth in there, smouldering,
and sometimes I see it
Break into a flame just for a second.

But at this time of morning
God often seems so far away
that he can't possibly hear me call.
It's then the doubts start crawling in
like some sort of rank weed
and set up house
in what I've come to call my soul.
Am I a sinner to feel this way?
I can hardly admit them to myself,
these doubts.
I'm scared
that if I name them,
they'll take solid shape
and overwhelm me.
Can't afford that.
I'm supposed to be so sure of everything.

So strong.
But sometimes I wish
I could just let go,
be my real and doubting self.
Because that's all we can hope to be.
I want to keep learning.
I'm just a man, after all.
A weak one.

Funny thing happened
on the way home last night.
That woman.
Ingrid.
I've seen her around.
They're new to town –
newer than I am.
You need to have been born here to be called a local.
I'm unsettled by Ingrid,
but why, I don't know. All I did
was help to get her car back on the road.
She seemed distant and close
at the same time.
Wonder what the story is there?
Everyone has a story.
Even Ingrid.
Even me.

And Mitch Larsen.
He didn't want to be seen in the car with me last night.
Not near town.
I think I understand,
but Ingrid Pallister must have thought it strange.

I think of the boy
who comes to sit in the back of the church sometimes.
Mr Emmerton's seen him, too.

'Want to watch that boy.
He's got darkie in him.
Be best if you lock the church except on Sundays.'

I was so shocked
to hear that word used these days
that I didn't ask him to elaborate.
There's no way
I'm going to lock a church in a small country town.
The boy's welcome.
Any time.
If he likes to sit in there,
that's fine with me.
I think it's great.
But do wonder about him.
Can't help it.
Maybe soon I'll go in there
and see if he wants to talk about something.
Won't matter what.

I'm actually in the church
when the lad comes in again.
I see him see me,
and turn to leave.
I almost let him go, but
something makes me say,
'Nic, isn't it? How are you?'
He's still walking towards

the open door
so I reassure him.
'Won't be a jiffy.
Just came to get a hymn book.
You're welcome to stay.'

He stops,
and keeps his schoolboy shoulders
hunched against me
for a few seconds.
Then turns.
'Thanks. I just like to sit, if that's okay.'

'That's fine. Any time you like,'
and go towards the side door.
'D'you like it here?' he asks.
'In Tillers Gap, I mean.'

'So far, so good,' I reply.
And then he sits down,
right where he is.
Again, something stops me from leaving.
I too sit.
And although there are rows
of bum-polished pews
between us,
we talk.
Awkwardly at first.
Nic tells me that his dad
used to come to church here.
That he just upped and disappeared months ago.
Funny how no one's mentioned it to me.

The boy is lonely, hurt
and angrier than he understands.
I don't ask much.
Don't have to,
because what he says
is enough for now.
Bright lad, year 10,
enjoys school, fishing.
Articulate,
but can't find the words
for his pain.
He tells me about his mum,
how she works all hours
at the community centre.
He doesn't know what she's thinking,
can't tell her what he's feeling,
but believes she blames herself
for her husband's leaving.
He talks on,
spreading out his story for me,
like a map I can read him by,
as if in the telling
he'll somehow find his way.

Then suddenly he stops.
'Shit! Sorry, sir,'
and I have to grin,
'I'm supposed to be at the vet's,
cleaning out the cages after school.
I am so late! See ya!'
And he's gone,
running up the street.

I come out and start to call him,
just to let him know he's welcome any time.
But his name falls
from my mouth.

Across the street,
astride her burbling red bike,
is that mailwoman.
She's watching me
with a smirk of satisfied malice
that's frightening.
Without greeting her,
I turn
and go back inside.
I hope the kid comes back
another time.

Beryl Anguis

My son Damon
has written 'Deliverence'
on the mudguard of my bike.
He's actually painted it on,
the twit.
Thinks he's funny,
like all seventeen-year-olds when they're not busy sulking.
I don't s'pose anyone here's
going to complain,
but it is meant to be
an official Australia Post vehicle
and it shows he still can't spell.
I gotta admit, though,
I kind of like it,
taking the mail around on my red bike,
except when it's been raining, like lately,
and I have to wear that ridiculous
plastic yellow raincoat.
Makes me look like a bloody preschooler.
I do the town run and about ten ks
on the road out to Larkin.
But for that I have to take my car
and slap on one of those magnetic labels
which makes me all official.

You sure get to see things
when you ride around this place.
Born and bred in Tillers Gap,
and stayin' here.
Learned a lot about people.
Some of it
from the mail I deliver,

some of it
from just keepin' me eyes open.
It's handy, knowin' things.
Real handy.

For instance, Meg Tulloch
doesn't always sleep at her own house.
Or let's just say she leaves her car outside Warren Robart's place
several times a week.
Nothin' wrong with that, except
Mrs R is away on one of them cruises
down some river in Europe.

I know that Ernie Coulter gets a parcel every month.
Brown paper, but in the corner
a little stamp says, 'Tickle your fancy'.
Didn't think they were allowed to do that –
y'know, put labels and things on
that gave them away.
Good for me, though.
Ernie knows I know,
and so he always serves me
the best cuts of meat.
There's no need to say anything,
just smile,
while Ernie lowers his eyes
to the sausages
under the glass counter.

On my rounds today
I saw Zoe Vandenburg
talking to that Nic Salter.

Mrs V won't like that,
not one bit.
Still hates Nic's dad
after all these years.
And now he's gone away...
Knew he wouldn't last.
Not with that woman.

Now my Damon,
he's a bit of a rough diamond,
but he's got a good heart.
I got chocolates for Mother's Day,
even though he ate most of them.
His dad was a loser.
Shot through when Damon was six
and the kid's been a handful ever since.
I was almost glad
when he was finally expelled from school.
Spat out, more like.
They always had me up there
for one thing or another.
They'd pick on him,
kids, teachers, every chance they got,
and he was always gettin' blamed
for things other kids would do –
'specially that Nic Salter,
come to think of it.
Just because his mum's Aboriginal,
Nic would get treated special.
All the excursions paid for, his uniform half price.
Wasn't fair.

There's lots of us findin' it hard.
Not just them.
I bet it was Nic stole the woodworking tools,
not my Damon.
He put them in our yard up behind the shed
just so Damon would get the blame.
That was the worst time.
The cops were called for that.
And Damon warned.

But Nic, of course,
was whiter than white.
Now there he is,
going into the church after school sometimes.
What good's a church?
Why the hell would he want to go there?
But I'll keep an eye on him.
And wait.

I could get Damon to watch,
if he'd stay home
long enough to talk to.
Comes in at all hours,
still asleep when I have to go out.
I know he goes to the pub.
And I know they serve him,
the fools.
He's not eighteen yet.
Don't know where he gets the money.
Wish he'd get himself a job,
but he just slopes around the place,
on the edges of trouble.

Somethin's gotta give
pretty soon.
But he's a good kid, really,
is my Damon.
I can prob'ly get him
to help me with a few things.

I'm riding past,
mindin' me own business
when I see that Nic run out of the church.
So I slow right down,
and take me time
snappin' the elastic band
on the next batch of letters.
I twang it a few times,
just testin',
as the boy belts along the footpath
across the street.
And then what do I spy with my little eye,
but that preacher come out.
He starts to call after Nic
but sees me and stops.
Turns and walks back
into the church.
Looks a bit sus to me.
There's a lot on telly these days
about priests and young boys and that.
Can't keep their hands off of them.
But here in Tillers Gap?
Can't believe it,
but he looked bloody guilty to me

slinking back
into his lair.
Gotta be somethin' queer there.
Don't like ministers,
or whatever they call themselves these days.
Maybe now Damon can earn his keep.
He's bored out of his mind,
but doesn't know it.
Buggers me what he does all day.
You'd think he had a real hectic,
high-falutin' lifestyle.
Even have to mow the lawn meself,
and he never does his own washing.
Still, he's young,
and I s'pose he needs to sow his wild oats.
Just hope
he's bloody careful.
And I can't figure
how come he never asks me for money?

Nic

I hate these days.
But my mother's the sort
who thinks everything
the school does
is just wonderful.
So she believes
that sports days are 'part of our overall development'.
What crap.
So here I am, on the hill,
which is actually a dusty bit of a slope near the running track.
It's colder than usual today,
but then that's what always
happens at sports carnivals.
If it rains at a swimming carnival,
they cancel the thing.
Tell me the logic in that!
I'm sitting on the edge of things
but close enough to others not to be noticed
by some watery-eyed,
coat-clutching teacher.

The sky's the colour of cheap cutlery.
Brass monkey weather my dad calls it
and I wonder why
when I say this to Old Philpott, he glares at me
and does his turkey neck impression.

We're supposed to wear house colours to these things,
but I'm buggered
if I'm going around town in yellow.
Not even here in Tillers Gap.

Have you noticed
how the sound of people calling out
is different in this weather?
It is, you know.
Kind of cold and sharp.

I'm looking around for Zoe,
but she doesn't seem to be anywhere.
I like her a lot
and think the feeling is reciprocated.
We had that word last week.
It's great. Reciprocated.
In the same lesson
we did 'unrequited'.
Like the word,
but don't want the situation.

Last week,
when we were on work experience
Zoe and I had lunch together most days.
It was great, 'specially when her friends didn't come.
Not that I did anything.
I'm not game.
Not yet anyway.
But I hope she meant the looks
she gave me – and the way
she didn't move her arm away
when I let mine
brush against it.
Her friends think
I'm a loser,
maybe because I actually enjoy school,

but I think it's more than that.
'A bit of the old tar brush.'
They don't actually say, and I know
they never will,
but it does sting a bit.
Zoe doesn't seem
to give a stuff.
One reason I like her.
I also happen to think
she's gorgeous –
that waterfall of hair, her giggle
and the way she walks.

That's when I realise where she might be.
She loves running, so maybe…
Yes, over there, lining up for some race.
Her hair's caught up in a ponytail.
She reminds me a bit of a filly
tossing her mane,
sort of skittish and eager for life.

Philpott's doing the announcing.
Fancies himself as a bit of a DJ.
He's 'enunciating his vow-els clearly',
and he sounds ridiculous.
This is sports day at Tillers Gap,
for God's sake, not the Commonwealth Games.
The year 7 drop kicks
are flitting around with messages
and the serious runners are warming up
and putting on spikes.

There are even some parents here
to see their darlings compete.
There's one mother behind me,
festooned in red house colours,
waving a stopwatch around
as if it's the Eureka flag.
Our school doesn't run
to a starting pistol – ha! Get the pun!
So some teacher's down there
dropping a flag like a stationmaster.
And they're off!
Must be quite a long race,
because even I can tell they're pacing themselves.
These girls are obviously serious about it all.
And then I see Zoe lope past below our hill
and despite myself,
my heart's chugging
like a steam train.
When she races by again,
I almost yell her name aloud.
It looks as though she comes in second,
and I'm disappointed for her.
The girls shake each other's hands.
Must be a big deal.
I've got no idea about these things.
Then Zoe's walking
off the track
and I lose her
in the chaos of kids
who always have to be down there
right in the action.
I so wanted her to win.

I slump back
and take out the book I'm reading
while there are no teachers around to stop me.
Ironic, isn't it?
Suddenly,
there's a pair of tanned legs in my vision.
Zoe.
'Hey, stranger,' she says,
and bends down to grab my book.
'What you reading?
Catcher in the Rye?
What's that about?
No, don't tell me,
I don't really care.'

And the next thing I know
Zoe's sitting down beside me,
beside Nic Salter!
She leans forward
and gathers her hair into one of those twisty things
and it brushes my face.
Her legs are bare
and goose-bumpy from the cold.
But I nearly melt
with a feeling I can't explain.
I can tell you I've got more
than a goose-bump going on,
and pull my knees up
to hide it.

This girl is doing things
to me that I've never felt before.
I'm uncomfortable
and excited
at the same time.
Then Zoe grabs my jumper
from where I've chucked it,
pulls it on over her shining hair,
and turns on her 100-watt smile.
I have to shift position again.
I'm sure she knows,
but all she says is,
'That's better.
You don't mind, do you?'

Mind?
Man, I'm over the moon here.
Sitting on the hill
with Zoe Vandenburg
beside me.
But as soon as Zoe leaves to race again,
the stirring starts.

'Hey, Nic!
Got yourself
a nice bit there, mate.
Didn't know she liked them dark, but.'
This is coming from behind me.
I know who's sitting there –
a bunch of blokes
from year 11.
But I don't turn around.

'Just ignore them,'
Mum always says.

But the awful truth is
they scare me.
I can tell they're jostling each other,
and hear them snort
like randy bulls.
After a while, they get bored
and stop baiting me.
My shoulders relax a bit,
until one of them gets
his second wind and starts with,
'Ooh, Zoe, darling, please be
my girlfriend. I want you so bad.'
Then more stupid noises,
trying to get me to react.
I've just about had enough
and start to get up
when Philpott does another 'turn of the grounds'.
Who'd have thought
I'd ever be glad to see
Old Philpott?

The noises are replaced by 'G'day, sir.
Enjoying the carnival?
We are, aren't we, Nicco?'
But at least I'm safe for now.

It's when the whole thing's over,
when they're happy enough
that we haven't left any rubbish,
year 7s, crepe paper

or sports equipment behind
that they let us go
with the usual reminders
not to make a nuisance of ourselves
down in the main street.

'You're being dismissed
earlier than usual today,
so don't let down the reputation of the school.'
As if reputations were in greater danger before 3 p.m.
And as if the school
had any sort of decent reputation anyway.

I'm one of the last to leave,
not because I like it there,
but because I'm up to a good bit in the book.
I stand, look around,
and realise how quiet it is.
No one much left,
except for a couple of teachers
dismantling the high jump in the middle of the oval.
And except for those year 11s.
They seem in no hurry to leave.
In fact, I think they're waiting for me.
How nice.
I try to look nonchalant, cool.
I'm good at this,
but my heart's hammering
and my hands go all clammy.
As I go to walk past,
one of them shoves me.
Another grabs my book.

'Whooee, what've we got here, boys?
The Cat-cher in the Rye.
Wonder what's it all about, Nicco?
Boy meets girl?
Boong meets girl?
You gunna read it to us?'
And they start chucking the book around.
I want them to keep doing that for ever,
while I edge myself towards the street,
hoping there'll be other people there.
No such luck.
They start jostling me from all sides.

'Hey, come on,
don't be such a spoil sport, Nic.
We're just havin' a bit of fun.
Whaddaya reckon about Zoe, eh!
Great tits, and those legs
go all the way up – and up.
Bet you'd like to put it up her,
wouldn't you, boong boy?'

That's when things actually go dark.
Something inside me explodes
and I hear my fist
connect with Tim Keesing's cheek.
Shit, it hurts,
but it must have hurt him too.
He reciprocates, and I taste
the blossom of blood in my mouth.
Now there are three of them on me,
my face is in the earth,

and something hard,
maybe a tree root, jabs into my ear.
They've twisted my arms up behind my back
like when the cops jump someone and arrest him.
Hurts like buggery,
but I try not to cry out.
They're making heaps of noise,
grunting, kicking at my legs,
but still no one comes.

Between thumps, one of them rasps,
'Where's your daddy gone, Nicco boy?
Couldn't stand any more black woman, eh?
Take this as a warning, darkie.
You hang around Zoe Vandenburg again,
and we'll have to spend
some time with her too.
Then she'll know
what real men are like.
We'll show her a good,
hard time.
Understand?'

I'm trying to form a tough-sounding reply
when there's a shout.
'Hey! What's going on there?'
and I'm turned over like a barbecue steak,
kicked once more in the nuts
and left alone.
I can hear them thudding off,
joshing each other,
happy lads all together.

I try to get up and pretend I'm fine.
Doesn't work too well.
For a start, I'm still quivering
with fear and rage.
I'm filthy,
there's grass and twigs in my hair,
my bloody mouth's puffing up
and my shirt's ripped.
It's Mr Vassallo, the PE teacher.
It would be.
He thinks I'm a loser anyway.

'What's going on, Nic?' he asks,
and I hear my voice mumbling,
'I'm fine, sir, really.
Just tripped, that's all.'

'Bullshit,' he replies.
(Mr Vassallo likes to think he's one of the boys.)
'Come on, who was it?'

'Don't know, sir. Didn't see them.'
I realise how pathetic I must look to him.
My lip's swelling already.
There's blood on my hands
from where I tried to break my fall on the gravel
and my legs are aching like a pensioner's.

Vassallo sighs and shifts the rope he's carrying.
'Don't be stupid, Salter.
I can't do anything about this
if you won't come halfway.'
He's impatient to get going.

Rattles his car keys
and tries to look pastoral.
He's shit at it.
He couldn't give a stuff.
Those year 11s are in his footy team.
And, despite what he thinks,
I'm not a complete moron.
I know the rules here.
So I play by them.

'No, really, sir.
It was just some boys.
We were mucking around.
No big deal. Honest.'

And Vassallo sighs again, trying to sound fed up,
but I can recognise a sigh of relief.
Means he can go to the pub with the other teachers,
and he won't have to follow up the incident
and write a report next week.
So, although he says, 'Not happy, Nic,'
he's lying through his whitened teeth.
'But I can't help you
if you won't help yourself.'

'Understood, sir.'
By now my lip has ballooned,
and my tongue finds a loose tooth.

'Well, you get yourself home and cleaned up.'

This is as close as Vassallo gets to caring.
He walks off,
the thick tug-o'-war rope scraping
along the ground behind him.
I lean against a camphor laurel
for a minute.
Even breathing hurts.
The place is deserted now
and I'm glad.
I feel really shaky,
whether with anger or shame,
it doesn't matter.
So I just stand, waiting for my body
to click back into position.

I try to walk as though nothing out of the ordinary
has happened, but I feel so obvious,
broken somehow.
Home's not far,
just two quiet streets away.
Lucky Mum's at some conference,
some community workers thing.
She won't be home until late.
I'm glad Zoe didn't see me
like this.

Beaten.

Mitch

Never thought I'd say it,
but I really like that minister.
He drove the thirty ks to the Larkin pub,
without asking why.
It's true I didn't want to be seen with him in Tillers Gap.
Not a good look,
me with a minister.
The pub at Larkin's a real old one,
and pretty run down.
People from Tillers Gap
hardly ever go there,
'cause it's a real one-horse, one-pub town,
and rough to boot,
but Tom wasn't fazed.
He seemed fine with it,
I'm sure no one could tell he was a priest.

Told him a bit about myself,
Suzy and the kids.
Suzy wasn't too happy
when I said I was going out for a drink.
Don't know what she'll say
when I tell her who I was with.
But I had a good time
and I did end up asking his advice
about the other night at work.
He listened as though he was really concentrating.
Tom's only been in Tillers Gap this year.
He used to be married,
but his wife died two years ago.
No mention of kids.
Much as my two drive me nuts

I wouldn't be without them.
Anyway, he'll do some research
about the mine overflow.
It hasn't rained for a while now,
so the pond should be okay.
Still, it's not something I can just let go.
But I know now
there's someone to share the problem with.

My next night shift was four days later.
I'd kind of shelved
what had happened the time before,
handed it over to Tom Shelley,
and there'd been no rain at all since then.
My job is to load and unload equipment
and move heavy machinery between yards.
I use a forklift or front-end loader most of the time.
It can be pretty boring,
except when I'm asked to help
fix some of the machinery.
I like that.
I do get to see what's going on
all over the place,
but a high-rise forklift ticket
is the only qualification I've got.
My boy Cam's impressed by that,
but he's alone there.
But it's good money, so I'm not complaining.

Me and Suzy want a bit of security behind us.
She does cleaning for a few places in town
but I don't like her having to work.

Mrs Huckstepp from next door
takes Carly when Suzy cleans.
Says it keeps her young.
She's a great old bird, Mrs H.
Lived next door
for as long as I can remember
and knew my mum and dad
and Brian and me
when we were kids.
But it seems kind of downgrading,
having my wife dust and vacuum
other people's rubbish and dirt.
She doesn't see it that way.

'I like it, Mitch,' she tells me.
'I get ideas about what we can do
to our place one day
and most of the people are really nice.'

Suzy cleans for the Untermeyer twins,
who must be near ninety by now,
the Osgoods (Mr O is a big shot at the mine),
and the Pallisters. They're new to town.
He's an accountant.
Seems a nice bloke.
Quiet, with an even quieter wife.

Anyway, here I was at work,
not thinking about much at all,
when Jake comes and says,
'What've you been up to, mate?'

'What you talking about?' I ask,
but already
there's a cool shiver
of uneasiness there.

'The supervisor was askin' about you.
Whether you were reliable and that.
I told him shit, yeah,
but he still didn't seem too happy.
Didn't ask any more.
Just walked off.'

'How come?' I asked Jake.

'No idea, mate.
It's prob'ly nothin'.
Don't worry about it, Mitch.'

And I said I wouldn't.
But I am worrying.
Can't help it.
What made it worse
was when I'd finished my shift
and was walking across the compound,
there he was –
the bloke from the other night,
just standing beyond the fence,
staring.
I'm pretty sure it was him,
though I wouldn't swear to it.
He didn't come over to me,
but nodded,
as if we had some agreement.

And as far as he was concerned,
I guess we did.
But I went home
not easy in myself.
Blokes have been laid off lately,
but that won't happen to me.
Will it?
Need to talk to Tom Shelley again.
See what's happening.
But I reckon he'll let me know
if he comes up with anything.

I had a dream last night.
Hardly ever dream
or, if I do, I sure can't remember.
But this one was awful.
In it, we'd driven out to the mine
and I was showing the kids around.
Suzy was hanging washing all over the car
while she waited for us.
Then I saw
the ground at our feet was wet
and we were standing in a puddle
that started to rise
and spread.
There were lots of ducks
but they were flailing and drowning.
Suzy was cranky because the rising water
would mean the washing wouldn't dry.
I was trying to get her to help me get the kids away
but all she could say was
'All that trouble for nothing'

as she plastered the roof of our car
with damp kids' clothes.
Man, was I glad to wake up,
and find Suzy gently snoring
beside me.

Zoe

Didn't see Nic until the Monday after the carnival.
His lip was all swollen and split.
It looked disgusting.
I'm not in any of his classes
and when I called out to him at recess,
he put his head down
and just kept walking.
We had assembly then
to give out the sports awards.
I got one for Most Successful Senior Girl.
Don't worry,
I won't let it go to my head.
After year 9, it's not cool
to take part in anything much,
and years 11 and 12 think it's positively daggy
to be enthusiastic about school.
Too bad. I love running –
all sports, for that matter.
I had to go up onto the stage to get a shield and cup.
People clapped, sort of,
but I could also hear my name whispered
and some pretty disgusting noises
coming from the year 11 area.
Don't know what I've done
for that to happen.
Don't even know most of them.
What are they on about?
Tried to see where Nic was,
so I could catch him outside.
Couldn't find him.
Was he ashamed of being seen with me?

Didn't think I was quite that daggy.
But then,
when we were leaving the assembly,
a year 7 boy snuck up to me
and pushed a note into my hand.
I opened it on the way to my locker,
It said, 'Can you meet me after school
in the park? N'
He must have meant where we had lunch last week.
I was glad he wanted to see me
and this was kind of romantic
Anyway, I wanted to give back his jumper.
I'd worn it for the rest of the day
at the carnival and I was home
before I realised I still had it on.
I stuffed it into my schoolbag.
Mum would have gone spare if she'd noticed it.

All day I'd been thinking about seeing Nic,
but when we met
he was really quiet,
almost sulky.
I was hoping he'd hold my hand,
maybe kiss me.
But he didn't even touch me.
I was so disappointed.
His lip was still swollen and puffy
and he had grazes down his cheek.
'What happened to you?' I asked.

'Don't worry about it. I'm fine,
I just need my jumper back.'
What he was saying just didn't seem right.
I pulled his jumper out of my bag
And started to say,
'Nic, I thought…'
but he cut me off.

'I'm sorry, Zoe, real sorry.
I'll see you around.'
He grabbed his jumper,
turned from me
and walked away.

I just stood there,
trying to get the hang of what had happened,
hoping he'd turn round
and look –
like he had last week.
Then I walked home.
Alone.

Must've been Thursday.
I was with Bree and Maddie after school,
when these older boys started following us.
At first we thought it was cool,
them wanting to talk to us,
but after a while
they got close enough
for us to hear what they were saying.
It was real scary.
They were muttering stuff
like 'Zoe Vandenburg needs teaching a lesson.'

And they were going to do it.
All of them.
Zoe's been hanging out with a boong,
which was a very bad idea,
and so Zoe needed to be shown the difference
between black boys
and white boys.
Before it was too late.

Bree was giggling at first
and then even she got scared.
The boys were getting closer
and closer.
Maddie was the one who finally did something.
She yelled, 'Piss off, you scumbags
or we'll tell Mr Hardwick,'
and she shoved
us ahead of her.
We made it to the shops
and sat in the hamburger place
to have a soft drink.
I still felt shaky,
but once things clicked into place
I was so angry.
I didn't tell the others
my thoughts.
Not yet, anyway.
They were too busy
making up reasons why we were being followed.
Couldn't they see?
By the time we'd had the last slurp,
Bree had decided that it was all cool again.

But I could tell
by the look she gave me
they hadn't fooled Maddie.

Nic

Sometimes I hate myself
almost as much as those yobs
seem to hate me.
Just when I find someone
who thinks I'm more than okay,
I go and stuff it up.
I dunno.
Guess Zoe can be added to the list of Nic-haters now.
With me at the top.

I find myself outside the church,
and it's open,
so I go in.
Started coming here just to sit, really.
Be on my own.
No footy players will come here,
and that new minister doesn't hassle me.
He didn't know about Dad,
how he used to come to church here.
Before.
Before what?
Wish I knew.
He's just not around any more.
Left nothing except a note saying,
'I will return.'
That was a joke just between us,
me and Dad.
Old Macarthur's words.
We'd find a reason to say it
to each other every few days.
But that was February 17th,
and he hasn't returned.

The cops reckon he's just gone off somewhere
to get away.
They didn't say from us
but I know that's what they think.
Because Mum's dark,
an Aboriginal.
As her son,
I must be also be simmering with trouble.
They didn't know my dad.
Not like I did. Do.
He has to come back.
Mum needs him.
And so do I.

Anyway, I'm sitting here
at the back of this little old church,
with the afternoon light
bleeding through the stained-glass window.
I can smell fresh flowers.
Don't know what they're called,
but they're around on Mother's Day.
These ones are yellow,
nice and bright.
I lean back and look at the ceiling.
Dark timber beams.
A cobweb drifting in the afternoon dust.
I just think about Dad
and wonder where he is
and if he's okay.
Because we're not.
We want him home.
I wouldn't tell Mum this,

but I sometimes try
to think him back to us.
How dumb is that?
But maybe if I concentrate hard enough,
he'll know we're still here,
still waiting,
still lonely.
Why would he leave?
He didn't do stuff like that.
'Happy John' everyone called him,
He'd lived in Tillers Gap all his life.
Where else would he go?
And not take me?
He's my dad.
He said he'd come back,
and he has to.
For me.
And for Mum.

I often ride my bike out to Deep Pools
'cause that was our place,
and look around.
Just in case.
I stare down, down
into the water
that seems a lot darker now
than it did when he was with me.

I'm coming across that bit of grass in front of the vet's
when I see them.
Damon Anguis has added himself,
and a noteworthy addition he is too.

Big D, they used to call him at school.
He thought it referred to his personality
and was quite proud of it.
Now he's here with the others,
the ones who stayed at school,
but no one knows why,
the ones who just thump around
even in classes
and don't seem happy
unless they're tackling or kicking someone
with or without a ball.
These are ones I'm scared of.
So I do the sensible
and cowardly thing
I run.

I get as far as the old Ferrier place –
empty now since they both died
in the fire that destroyed
a lot of the house as well.
I find myself charging
up the scorched front stairs
and through the already
open door.
The house stinks.
Piss and cigarettes and vomit,
something dead and more piss.
Somehow this registers
before I feel myself crashing
through the burned floorboards in the old kitchen.
Luckily, the ground isn't too far down
and my jeans protect me a bit.

My ankle twists over
and I rip another shirt.
There I stand,
like an idiot,
stuck up to my waist
in a hole of my own making,
hearing the thudding footfalls close in on me
down the narrow hallway.
What can I do?
Stupidly, I try humour,
hoping to put them off balance.
'Can I help you fellas?'
my voice quivering
as much as my legs.
I want to pee.

'Well, lookee here. Just waiting for us,
were you, black boy?
Didn't you think
we meant what we said, Nicco,
about not seeing that girl,
that Zoe Vandenburg?
We asked you nicely the first time.
We might have to show
that we mean it now.
She's too good for you,
Can't have you gettin' your greasy mitts over her.
Didja think we wouldn't find out
about your secret meeting
in the park, eh?
Swapping school jumpers and all.
How cute is that!

We told you
what might happen to Zoe babe.
Now we're gunna have to
teach you a lesson too.
Never mind, we'll keep it simple.'
And goon number one
turns to goons two, three and four.
'Okay. Who wants first go?'

I try to lever myself
out of this ragged hole in the floor,
but no doing.
I'm hunched over
as one of them starts kicking at my shoulders and arms.
Next thing, it'll be my head.
You see this sort of thing on TV
when some poor bloke,
usually a police informer, is caught by the baddies
and gets the life belted out of him.
But this is surreal
and part of me separates,
to float above,
watching it all happen.
Luckily these blokes aren't that desperate,
and I don't think they'll kill me,
but it doesn't feel too good.
I shut my eyes.

The sound becomes magnified.
It's a hard sound –
fist on flesh
and there's the grunting accompaniment.

I crouch down
and realise if I judge it right,
I might be able to roll to one side,
so that I'm still under the floorboards,
but not as easy a target.
I give it a go.
It works.
There's dust and cobwebs
in my mouth and I smell mouse shit,
but they can't get me here,
not unless they come down after me,
one by one.
Even they've worked that one out.

Someone, I think it's Anguis,
sticks his head down through the opening
and I manage a clumsy punch at it.
'You little fuckwit…'
but he withdraws.
The others have gone outside
to see if they can get at me from there,
but there's lattice
nailed all around the underside of the house.
Now I've got an advantage,
but try telling my body that.

Ingrid

I should have worked out
how to get this pullover back
to Bible-thumper by now,
but I haven't.
It's a nice jumper,
a bit lighter than royal blue and cabled,
made with skill and love.
She'll be asking him about it.
There's the op shop run by the church.
Maybe I can find out in there.
But I don't want people seeing,
thinking I need to go to an op shop.
Clive makes sure
I never need for anything.

Wanting is altogether different.
Clive is frightened
I have someone else in Sydney.
I don't,
but I'm not going to disabuse him of that notion
just yet.
My old boss, Neil,
has said after too many,
too long lunchtime meetings
he's there if I ever 'need him'.
But that's not it.
Sometimes I don't know what I want,
but it's not a security blanket
sort of man, that's for sure.
Perhaps I'm still yearning
for the child that never was.

Here I am
sitting in the bedroom
holding this jumper to myself
as if its warmth will cure the restlessness in me.
I pull it on over my clothes
and lie on the bed,
hugging myself as if the day was very cold.
It can't possibly still smell of him,
but it does.
I fall asleep there,
on top of the made bed,
where Clive later finds me.
I wake with a start
sensing him as he leans over me.

'Are you okay, Ingrid?' he asks,
peering through the shuttered gloom.
Solicitous as ever, is Clive.
'Do you have a headache?
Can I get you something to for it?'
God, I wish he could.
But I mumble nothings
and rise to get him a cup of tea.
That's what he really came looking for.
He wouldn't have noticed the pullover.
but I made sure to take it off.
before filling the kettle.

Clive

I found her mid-afternoon
on the bed.
Not like Ingrid at all.
I'm not complaining.
Just that it's unusual,
and we normally have a cuppa at three-thirty.
I watched her for a minute
before speaking.
Seems the only chance I get now
to look directly at her.
She was huddled there
looking really vulnerable.
I was going to get a rug
and then noticed she was wearing a jumper,
one I hadn't seen, blue and bulky.
She must have bought it in Sydney.
Her hair had come loose
and some was trapped
under the pullover.
I leaned forward,
yearning to touch hair,
touch her.
But that's when she woke with a start.

We sit on the veranda with our tea and biscuits.
Unsaid words fall through
the space between us,
broken and brittle.
Ingrid reads
The Sydney Morning Herald.

Mitch

Me and Suzy were sitting out on the veranda.
Cam was watching *Ice Age*
for the hundredth time,
and Carly was sound asleep at last.

Suze said to me,
'Mitch, you know when the minister came here
and you went to the pub?'

'Yeah,' I said, 'what about him?
He's a good bloke, Suze.
You'd get on well.'

'It's not that,' she said.
'Just something funny I saw at Pallisters' today.
Funny peculiar, I mean.
Probably nothing.'

Really bugs me when she does that,
leaves things hanging,
like someone who won't tell you the punchline to a joke.
She wants me to ask,
so I say, 'What are you on about?'

'Well, it's just that…
Y'know that blue jumper he had on
when he came to the door – the minister?'

'Don't ask me what he was wearing.
I suppose he had a jumper on. Why?'

'I'm probably imagining things,
but I noticed it because it was a real nice blue
and was hand-knitted.
I was thinking,
wish I could do that…'

'Come on, Suzy, cut to the chase here.'

'Well, today, when I was cleaning at Pallisters',
I vacuumed under the bed
and saw the same jumper
folded behind the bed head.
Can't see how it could've got there.'

'Come on, babe, there's no way it would be the same one.
I'm pretty sure Tom had never spoken to the lady
before he helped with her car.
I told him what I knew about them
on the way home,
and I only know the things you've said.
Forget about it.
There'd be nothing dodgy going on there.'

'You're probably right'
was her answer,
and she tucked her hair behind her left ear
in that cute way she has.

But I know the signs.
Suze'll mull over that jumper thing
like a bit of meat caught between her teeth.
She went to run Carly's bath
while I finished my cigarette.

The smoke rose like a question mark.
I stubbed it out and went
to kneel beside the bath
and wash my little girl.

Ingrid

I've done it.
I've joined something.
A quilting group.
There was an article about them in the local paper.
They were donating a quilt to be raffled for the hospital,
and it said they were looking for new members.
The ladies in the photo looked older than me,
but I thought if I don't do
something outside myself
I'll go mad in this place.

When I shop, everyone smiles at me
as if they know me,
or at least
know something very interesting
about me,
which can be quite unnerving.
But no one knows enough
to stop and talk.
Not sure that I want them to.
The whole thing seems a bit too *Country Living* to me.

The quilting group meets in the church hall.
I thought,
what if I see him?
I've still got his pullover.
What if his wife's in the group?
What if she's the alpha female?

As it turned out,
it wasn't like that at all.
The hall was the original church

and has a polished timber floor.
It's airy without that musty smell
that often loiters in churches,
and clergy for that matter.
There are a few religious posters
and some notices about 'Mission'
but it seems the community use the hall
as much as the church members.
There's a bit of a kitchen at one end
where everyone – except me –
deposited homemade offerings for morning tea.

The ladies were really nice,
and although I was right about their ages,
it didn't matter.
There was one other 'newie'
who seems a bit younger than me.
I was prepared for the inevitable question session,
but they weren't too intrusive
and I had answers I'd prepared earlier, as it were.

Fiona, the other new person,
brought a quilt she'd already started,
so I'm the only one
who's a true beginner.
Most of them were sewing quilts for family members,
and they vied with each other
to help me get started.
I felt welcome,
enveloped almost.
Some of the ladies don't seem to worry
about how much sewing gets done.

As long as there's some fabric in their laps
and a needle threaded,
they just sit there and chat.
One of them even brought her dog,
an old bitser,
who snored on a faded quilt under the table.
I've been sworn to secrecy,
because the dog's not supposed to be there.
It's nice to be included
in such a delightful conspiracy.
How anyone could object to Maisie's presence
is beyond me.

'Oh, it's not the minister,'
Mrs Someone (call me Denise)
leaned over and whispered loudly.
'It's that church secretary.
Self-righteous prig he is, begging your pardon.'
Soft laughter followed.
'The minister, Tom Shelley,
he's real nice. Comes in sometimes.
Just to say hello, you know.
He smiles and says,
"Give Maisie a pat for me when you see her."'

'He's a breath of fresh air, that one,'
added Nita from across the table.
'Lost his wife, poor man.'

My earlier panic
at the thought of Tom Shelley appearing
and requesting his jumper vanished.

I was shocked,
and felt as though I had been left out,
excluded from something vital.
I felt a jab of sympathy,
simultaneously wondering
whether said lost wife had knitted The Jumper.
Now at least I knew a bit about him.
But wanted more.
Maybe next week?
I like the sound of 'next week'.

Fiona even said to me,
'We must have coffee some time.'
Don't know that I'm ready
for a close encounter of the rural kind,
but it was nice to be asked.
I've done an important thing today,
and I'm glad.
There's something
to look forward to.
I'm going to enjoy choosing patterns and fabrics
for my own project.

At home,
Clive was wandering around
as if he too had lost a wife
and didn't know where to find her.
Impatience and nostalgia rose
in equal measure,
but then I saw
he'd not had morning tea
on his own,
and irritation won.

Why does he do this?
I've a good mind
to get up to something interesting,
just to make his anxiety concrete
I might as well, if I'm going to be suspected of it.
Clive sort of 'droops' around
the place as if he's permanently
ducking for cover,
his tall, skinny frame
buckled under some sort
of inward pressure.
I needed time on my own
to savour my morning.
I wish he was like Maisie the dog
and just kept out of the way a bit more.

He'd asked me about the dent
in my bumper bar.
You can't see it
until you get really close,
but trust Clive to notice.
I said I couldn't remember,
and he didn't push me on it.
It wasn't always like this,
and I can't put my finger on
how things have changed.
Wish there were some friends here –
even one – to talk to.
But it takes years
to get to that level with someone.
Mind you,
even my Sydney friends say

it's bound to be hard adjusting
because we've made the move from the city.
I'm not so sure.
I took myself down to the shops
to buy the bits and pieces for my quilt.
The main street here in Tillers Gap
is broad, wider than a lot of Sydney streets.
No traffic lights, just a couple of
unnecessary speed humps.
People drive at 40ks, windows down
so they can call out to those on the footpaths.
You'll hear 'Hey, mate!
When you gunna come and fix me pump?
Bin waitin' for days.'
Or 'I'll be there in a sec, Gwen.
Just had to get the washing out.'

You can get most things you need,
and once they know you at Todaze Fashions,
can take the clothes home to try on.
I haven't been inducted to that club yet.
There are two decent cafés,
and one that's firmly anchored in the 60s;
still with laminex tables
and vanilla slice as Cake of the Day.
I quite enjoyed myself.

I still want to make a full double quilt,
despite the complexity.
I had to get a tool called a rotary cutter,
a cutting mat, special ruler
and new, sharp scissors.

It was great fun selecting the fabric.
They have these squares called 'fat quarters' –
neat bundles of gorgeous designs,
just for patchworking.
I was a schoolkid again,
choosing colours for the embroidery project.
My first attempt will be
what's called a Pieced Sampler Quilt.
It looks fairly straightforward.
When I hear the other names
like Floating Four Patch
and the Jane Austen pattern,
I realise what a beginner I am.
But I'm happy
to be starting something new,
something fresh.
In the end I chose a simple pattern
that goes from dark to light.

Zoe

My computer's stuffed,
so I had to go to the library last night after dinner.
Don't go there often,
'specially at that time,
but we were doing a study on the book
To Kill a Mockingbird,
so we had to find out a whole lot of stuff
about the time, the place and all that
so we're able to 'fully appreciate the text'.
What a load of crap.
Still, I like the book a lot
and didn't mind the assignment.

The library was practically deserted,
a few old men
who'd found a place of escape,
or maybe they were just lonely.
Anyway, I was using one of the computers
when I thought I saw Nic
over in the corner,
browsing a row of books.
He hadn't noticed me,
so I watched him for a while.
I could only see parts
of him at a time,
like one of those kids' books
with three flaps you can change
so that you might get a hairy-legged nurse wearing a tiara.
I made sure
no one was waiting for my computer,
saved my work, went to the end of the row
and just stood.

After a few seconds,
Nic sensed something
and looked my way.
Nic has quite a big gap between his front teeth
which he tries to hide when he smiles.
This time he didn't bother.
I knew then I'd been right.
He still liked me – a lot.
But by the time I got to him,
he was frowning again.
I put my hands on his shoulders
and kissed him –
just softly
on his sore mouth.

Surprised even myself,
but Nic dropped the book
he'd been holding and hugged me.
He clung to me,
his face in my hair.
He smelled of Pears soap.
It was one of those
'time stood still' things, really.

Eventually, he said, 'Zoe.'
Just the one word.
Again, 'Zoe, we can't…'
I was about to say
something stupid
when he said, 'I mean,
we mustn't be seen together.
They'll hurt you.'

Like some sort of sick kaleidoscope
the bits fell into place.
The assembly, those yobs,
the stalking, the fat lip.
I was fuming.
'I'll see who I want, Nic Salter,
and it happens to be you.'

'You can't, Zoe,' he replied.
We found some comfy chairs in the corner,
and Nic told me everything.
When he'd finished,
I was even more angry,
but knew he was right.
We had to think of something.

Tom

Last night I dreamed Jen and I went on a picnic.
One perfect day.
We were so young,
so beautiful,
even me.
Everything we needed
was laid out before us
on a huge white cloth that covered a paddock.
As well as the food,
jacarandas scattered their purple flowers
and a gentle lion licked up the blossoms
with a dainty red tongue.
Over in the far corners of the sheet,
other couples were also picnicking,
signing to each other,
silently smiling.
We were the only ones who made a sound.
Jen laughed as she fed me,
murmured as she kissed me,
whispered as she stroked me.

Then suddenly
dark birds came,
snatched the cloth in their beaks,
whisked it from under us
and tore it away
up into a lowering sky.
We were left hungering,
silent.
Bereft.

When I woke,
my throat was dry with longing.
Yet I have to walk around this pretty town
being The Minister,
the one who knows things,
the one who has greater access.
To what? I want to ask.
I had to do a funeral yesterday.
Didn't know the man.
Had never heard of him before.
But there he was, tidily tucked
into a polished walnut coffin.
bedecked with red roses,
a flag and a photo of his younger self.
Predictably, they wanted
the twenty-third psalm,
and I said the expected things about a good innings,
good life, good mate.
The family seemed satisfied
with my performance,
and crossed my palm with more than silver
'…for the building fund'.
We have no need of new structures.
That's not what's missing.

I wonder how Nic's going?
Haven't seen him for some days now.
Hope I didn't scare him off.
Should I check up on his mother,
just to see how she's travelling?
Don't think that's what Nic would want.

Saw Mitch across the road last night.
He gave me a wave,
but then turned
and went inside his home.
I am lonely.

Nic

Zoe had to practise for the cross-country,
so we decided to meet
out at Deep Pools.
It was already special to me,
because of Dad,
and now it was to be our secret.
I often rode out there
after I'd done my work at the vet's.
No one gave a damn where I was,
and it was good thinking time.
I admit that at first I was sure
I'd see some sign of Dad out there.
I looked everywhere,
really hard,
frantic with loss.
But after a while,
you don't expect to find what you want.
So the intensity,
the panic, has gone,
leaving a constant, dull ache.

The wheels of my bike were still spinning
where I'd leant it against a rock
when I saw Zoe.
She came from the east
and was lit up like a lovely flame,
her long hair
tied back and swishing.
Her legs bronzed in the late sun.
But it wasn't just the bright light that made my eyes water.
Zoe kept running, right into my arms,

just like the movies,
just like my dreams.
And for that moment,
I was completely happy.
I gave her some water from my flask,
and she tipped
the rest of it over her head.
I kissed her then, properly,
wet mouth against dry,
until we were both wet.
Then we sat,
safe
in the bum-sized dent of a granite boulder,
warmed by the sun,
just holding each other.

I wanted to stay like that,
but Zoe said, 'Nic, we have to sort this out.
Somehow.'
I knew she was right,
but didn't want to spoil what we had
right there and then.

Beryl Anguis

I take me time,
workin' out what to do
about that minister bloke.
I don't really think
he's a paedo,
'cause Nic Salter's a big kid
and they usually like 'em younger.
Still, never did like
Bible-bashers.
Me grandad was a real churchy type,
and the stories Mum used to tell
showed him
as a real mean bugger.
Only got a coupla photos left,
and in them
he stands there,
his hands on Gran's shoulders
as if he's pressin' her down,
makin' sure
she doesn't crack a smile.
So Grandad,
it's all your fault
that I hate these Born Agains.

Yesterd'y I saw Mrs Beattie
in her front yard.
(She's always up at that church.)
I said, 'How's things goin', Lorna?
How's that minister of yours shapin' up?'
Mrs Beattie pulled herself straight
from kneeling
on her weeding mat,

and still holdin' her trowel
gave me a right going over
with those denim blue eyes of hers.
'He's just fine, thank you, Mrs Anguis.
He's a good man.
Is that my mail?
I won't keep you.
You must have a lot to get through.'

Well, I know a snub when I see one.
Old bat.
But I don't give up so easy.
'Is he thinkin' of startin'
one of those Boys Brigade things?'

Mrs Beattie had been sifting through her letters,
but I had her now.
She looked up, frowning.
'Boys Brigade? What on earth do you mean?'

'Oh, it's just that I seen that Salter boy
come out of the church a few times,
and the minister after him.'

'Well, I've heard no talk
of any young people's groups,
and what Tom Shelley does
is up to Tom Shelley.'
And she says again,
'He's a very good man.'
I straddled the bike
and walked it along past Mrs Beattie's house.

Her wire fence was already humming.
A good morning's work.
Just a couple more deliveries like that
should be enough.

Tom

I've just remembered where my pullover is.
I gave it to Ingrid Pallister
to hold
while I checked out her car.
It's been a while now,
and she hasn't brought it back.
Mind you, I didn't even realise it had gone.
I should've.
It's one of my favourites.
Jen knitted it for me.
Her hands were always busy.
Beautiful hands.
I've still got four jumpers she made me.
I don't wash them properly,
just throw them in the machine,
but they don't look too bad.
I'll wear them until they fall off me.
Wonder if Ingrid Pallister knits?
How should I go about getting my jumper back?
Don't like to just turn up and say,
'I think you have a piece of my clothing.
May I have it back?'

Unusual woman.
Gave off a sense of 'otherness',
of disappointment.
Something about her has lodged in my head
after a few minutes together in the near-dark.
Her perfume?
Her voice?

Not sure,
but she intrigues me.
I don't think Tiller's Gap
is awash with such women.

I must make some time
to check out the area around this town.
Should be some good walking tracks
and the hills look great for a bit of clambering.
Maybe Mitch would enjoy that sort of thing.
But he's got his family.

I wonder if Nic Salter would like to go for a hike
in the school holidays?
I'll ask next time he comes into the church.

Mitch

When I think about work,
it always has to do with making money.
It's not that I hate my job,
but it is just that – a job.
When they call it
clean coal,
it's not exactly true.
Is there any such thing?
Words like washing, grading, loading,
are now part of my world,
They're also part of Suze's world
when she's working in the laundry at home.
Coal straight from the ground, the run of mine,
has lots of impurities.
These end up
in a coal slurry pond –
or impoundment.
That word
'slurry', the blackwater,
is what worries me.
Can't see that mining's bad in itself,
God knows we need fuel.
It's just the huge mess it makes
and where it ends up.
Can't be good.
So I've taken to keeping an eye on the pond.
It hasn't rained for a while.
I know I'm being watched
but I'm starting to think,
be buggered.
I'm not doing anything wrong.

Show me
where my work's no good.
For now, I think
they're just watching me
watching them,
across the compound,
through the wire.

Need to go and see Tom Shelley again.
The man must get a bit lonely.
He had a letter in the local paper last week,
saying how we need to be careful with the land
that's been – I think he said 'entrusted' to us.
Some of his old fogies
won't be happy with that.
They won't rock any boat,
no matter what its flag or cargo.
Me, I like to think
I'm an independent sort of bloke.
But is there any such thing?
Suze is often telling me
to say what I think,
(to say what she thinks, maybe!)
but it's not that easy.

Gee, she's good value.
Yesterday she went off
to visit her mum, who lives in Blackheath,
so it was just me and the kids.
I think she should be paid more than me.
Cam was at school, or should have been.

At eleven, I get this phone call
to come and fetch him 'cause he's sick.
So I tear off to pick him up,
with Carly screamin' blue murder
in the back 'cause I'd grabbed a toy off her,
and there he is,
waitin', lookin' pretty healthy to me.
I reckon it was just that I was minding them.
He wanted to be with me.
I tried to get cranky,
but couldn't do it.
Actually, I was pretty chuffed.
That is, until Carly started
her bawling again,
and he wouldn't leave my side.
I'd told Suze, no worries,
the washing would be done,
the house tidy and even tea ready
when she got home.
Wondered why she gave me one of those smiles.

By the time she came back,
Carly was finally asleep
on my stomach.
I was sprawled on the lounge
with Cam at my feet, his uniform filthy.
happily stuffing his face with Cheezels
while on TV *Jamie's Got Tentacles* gave way to *Prank Patrol*.
The washing was still in the machine
and the house was trashed.
So was I, for that matter.

I know some blokes have partners
who'd let rip if they came home to that.
Not Suzy.
She gets cranky when she's tired,
but after a day away,
she just looked at us
and laughed out loud.
'You're a hopeless lot, aren't you?' she said,
peeling the sleeping Carly from my stomach
and sending me
to buy fish and chips.
I'm a lucky guy.

Clive

Ingrid seems almost happy.
Today she went to some sort of sewing group,
and she's come home
with all these bits and pieces.
I can hear her
singing to herself
in the spare room.
I'm glad something has made her smile.
Wish it had been me,
but if it's a new hobby that's good too.

I found myself knocking on the open door
to ask if she wanted a cup of tea.
I had annoyed her,
interrupted something private,
but it was too late.
'No, thank you.'
She didn't want anything from me.
Then she must have felt bad,
and for a minute
the other Ingrid returned.
'Come and see this, Clive.
I'm going to make a quilt.
Do you like the fabrics?
Nice, aren't they?'

'Beautiful,' I replied,
but I was looking at her.
She blushed and turned away
laying down more squares.
It'll be a wonderful quilt
of light and dark shades

when she puts it together.
I had the tea on my own,
but she had sung
and she had smiled,
even if not at me.

Beryl Anguis

Finally caught the boy last night.
He said he was off out.
I said, 'Enough's enough, Damon.
You're stayin' right here
until I know what's goin' on.
I'm sick of doin' your washin', cookin',
and cleanin' up after you
and bein' told bugger all.'

Didn't expect him to say much,
but maybe he was glad to be forced.
Once he got goin', he went on and on,
about how these blokes at the pub
are gettin' him to do things for them.
'Jobs', he calls them,
but I dunno about that.

Turns out,
there are two things goin' on.
Some blokes are shiftin' stuff
that's been nicked from all around.
Small things, mostly,
but some worth a bit.
Things from places that are vacant
after people have died, or moved on.
These blokes go in
and take what they want
before the auction people get there.
Bits of jewellery, silver,
antiquey stuff.
They need a place for storage
until the heat dies down.

My Damon has been stashin' loot for them
in some old mine shaft
out near Deep Pools.
It's safe there, he reckons.

I tell him,
'Nothin's safe.
You don't muck around
with blokes like that.
Once they've gotcha,
they've gotcha.'
I shake me head.
Sometimes I wonder where his brains are.
'Damon,' I said, 'son,
you're an idiot.
You're in with a bad lot
and now you know things.
They're not gunna let you go.'

'But Mum,' he tells me,
'they're good blokes.
They give me money for what I do.'

'Oh, that's why you're rollin' in cash, is it?
Why you're buyin' us a new house?
What am I gunna do with you, boy?'

'Nothin', Mum, please
don't do nothin'.
I can look after meself.'

Famous last words,
I reckon, but I need time
to think this one through.
God, who'd have kids?
One minute they're getting teeth,
the next they're up to the neck in trouble.
This is bad,
but one thing, my job's good for
is thinkin' and watchin'.
Ridin' around, you can
sort out lots of things
and people.

Tom

Two things have happened.
Not much in themselves,
but something's not quite right.
Yesterday, after service
Mr Emmerton bailed me up
as he does.
'What's this I hear about a Boys Brigade, Tom?'
I had no idea what he was on about,
and said so,
but Charles Emmerton was undeterred.
'I believe you're starting one.
Bit high-handed, I'd say,
without reference to Council.'

I assured him that nothing
was further from my mind.
(I'd had enough of such 'healthy
organised activities' when I was a kid.)
When I pushed
for the source of his wisdom, however,
I met a blank wall.

'Using that Salter boy
is what I hear,' he went on.
'Watch yourself there.'
And with that he was gone,
little grey wife in his slipstream.

I kept shaking hands, smiling,
and no one else made reference
to boys of any kind.
But it had left me unsettled.

Then the second thing.
The same afternoon
I took myself over
to Mitch's place to ask
if he'd like to go for a drink.
Suzy answered the door
and I could have sworn
she looked wary.
There was a footy game full blast on TV
and somewhere inside
the boy was yelling 'Hey, look at this!'

'Mitch isn't here right now,' she said.
'I'll tell him you called.'
It seemed a bit formal
and stilted.
Maybe I'm paranoid,
but I don't know many women
who'd watch the footy without a man there.
And who was the kid
talking to?
I left them alone.
Together.

Mitch

I heard the doorbell,
but the game had gone into extra time
so I let Suzy answer it.
After the Panthers had scraped a win, I asked,
'Who was that at the door?'

'The minister,' she said,
as she folded the washing.
'I told him you weren't here.'

'Why'd you do that?'

'Well, you hate having the footy interrupted.
I thought you'd be pleased.'

That wasn't like Suzy at all.
She never lied.
'Suze…' I began.
'Why didn't you…?
It's that jumper, isn't it?
Come on, I told you. He's a good bloke.'

Suze just looked at me,
a towel held up against her chest.
I knew then
she was becoming wary.
Doubtful.

Nic

I was dreaming.
We were out at Deep Pools.
There were birds circling,
black ones,
hundreds of them,
bigger than crows,
coasting, soundless.
The silence was absolute.
Dad and I were fishing, but our lines tangled
and we had to pull them in.
The water was black and viscous, like tar,
so that our lines dragged.
On the end of each was a bird
like the ones in the sky, only
these were nearly dead,
and gulped for air like fish.
They had both feathers and scales that were
clogged with oil.
I turned to Dad,
so that he would tell me what to do,
but he was gone.
When I looked up,
he was flying with the heavy birds
in dark circles.

Beryl Anguis

Damon told me
where he stashes the things
those men give him.
He rides my old motorbike out
towards Deep Pools.
He says he has to crawl into an old shaft
that burrows into a small hill.
There's a gate
and a padlock across the entrance.
Damon has the key
and he hides the things as far in as he dares go.
He reckons it's real dry in there,
so the silver and stuff won't spoil.
It's all wrapped up in cloths.

I don't like it.
Not one bit.
Anything could happen.
That gate's there for a reason.
To keep out fools
like my son.
Those old shafts can be dangerous,
what with rock falls
or even collapsed beams.
God knows what creatures,
maybe even snakes will be there.
Damon seems to think it's all 'A Boy's Own Adventure'.
I'm scared for him.

Think I'd better visit the pub,
something I haven't done much
since that loser of a husband shot through.

It's his old pub,
used to be his second home.
But it's time
for me to find out
what's really going on.

Ingrid

Something has shifted
in me.
I have a task.
A small purpose.
I've sorted out which patterns, which squares,
to put together my for my quilt.
It's really a matter
of working away at it,
of building up the design
bit by bit
until the colours blend as they should.
The pattern I've chosen
isn't as hard as it looks.
I think it's a good one
for a start.

Tom

Nic was there this afternoon,
when I went into the church.
He seemed pleased
to see me.
He was the first to sit down,
as if he needed to talk.
I was glad of it.
We spoke in circles for a while, but
got to the hub of things in time.

Turns out
Nic's being hassled by some older boys.
He's a tall, strong lad,
but hates organised sport.
It all seems to boil down to the fact that his mum's
Aboriginal,
and he's got himself a girl,
Zoe Vandenburg.
The name means nothing to me,
but apparently her mum isn't keen on them being together,
and may even
have put a word in the ear of some other year 11 mothers.
Seems they were only too happy to oblige.

Nic's also seen as a bit of a swot.
Put these things together
and you've got a victim
and some mindless bullies.
Nic didn't want me to interfere,
I think he just needed to talk.
But I can't just sit here.
This isn't right.

It won't stop
unless someone does something.
Who else will act?
Nic told me about this Zoe,
how strong she is,
how lovely.
The kid's head over heels.
and I'm glad for him.
If ever someone needed a good thing in his life.
Nic says Zoe's a bit of an athlete,
and does cross-country.
When I mentioned a bushwalk or climb,
he seemed keen,
and asked if Zoe could come too.
Sounds good to me.

He wants to show me Deep Pools,
where he and his dad used to go.
I'm humbled to think
he wants to share such a place
with me.
He and Zoe meet out there.
So we plan to go next week.
Then in the school holidays
the three of us will go on a proper bushwalk.

This time, after Nic left,
I sat there in the quiet,
grateful
for these crumbs of friendship,
hoping for real bread soon.
I knew I had to make a move on Nic's situation,

and help somehow.
But for now,
the small building seemed to settle around me,
almost like home,
almost like peace.
This morning I have to meet
with the new accountant
who'll do the books for the church.
The Council have had to find someone
because Ted Stevens, who's done
the books for aeons, has retired.
Good on him.

The chosen one
is a man
by the name of Clive Pallister.
This should not worry me.
His wife has my jumper –
has had it for some weeks.
That's all there is to it.
Surely?

Ingrid

Clive doesn't ask for much these days,
but he has asked
if I'll stay around this morning.
He has a new client,
one of the churches,
and the minister is coming to see him.
One Tom Shelley.
Clive thinks it would be nice
if we had morning tea with Reverend Shelley
after they've been through the books.
My first thought?
I haven't washed his damn jumper.
My second thoughts?
Well, they're a bit
of a jumble
but they include
such serious concerns as
does my hair look okay
and what should I make to eat?
I am ridiculously nervous.

Clive

Well now, that was interesting.
Tom Shelley seems
a really nice person.
The accounts are in a bit of a mess
but that's easily fixed, and not his fault.
He's been in Tillers Gap only this year.
Came from Victoria.
He's easy to talk to,
and once the accounting was sorted,
I found myself
telling him about our own move
to Tillers Gap from Sydney,
and how it hasn't been a resounding success.

Turns out
he feels much the same sometimes,
but lately has found a degree
of stability.
I realise now,
he's the one who wrote about the impact of mining on the town.
So he's not afraid
to give his opinion.
Ingrid had outdone herself.
Madeira cake, ginger slice and plunger coffee.
I was proud
to be her husband.
She hardly said a word at morning tea,
but she was there.
That was enough for me.
It was only when Tom was going
that he looked right at Ingrid and said,
'I'm just wondering. My…'

and she finished the sentence for him,
'…jumper. Yes, I'm sorry.
I wanted to wash it.
I'll get it to you ASAP.'
Now, that was an exchange
that left me
completely in the dark.

I didn't comment,
but when the door had closed,
leaving us
alone,
together,
Ingrid turned to me and said,
'Clive, I need to explain.
Can we have another cup of tea?'

Ingrid

Something broke in me,
and the tears came
in front of Clive for the first time in ages.
I told him about the jumper,
how I came by it,
and before I knew it
had blurted out the lot:
about not wanting to leave Sydney,
how it hurt, how I missed my job,
my friends, my suburb.
I cried very noisily,
and very messily,
and reproached Clive
for a great many unrelated failings.
But I needed to be allowed
to accuse,
even falsely.
So I spent some time
doing just that.

At first Clive sat
quiet and still
opposite me,
coffee mug in hand,
looking pained and bewildered.
Then just as I wept my way
to a crescendo of complaints,
I found him beside me,
his arm around my shoulders,
holding me firmly,
saying nothing,
just 'claiming' me again.

At first I relaxed into him,
remembering how good it felt,
how safe.
But then I pulled away.
I felt heavy,
coated in guilt.
What had I been saying?
That my husband was weak,
useless, boring and quite a bit more.
That I hated my life here,
it was his fault,
and I didn't think I could go on.
Eventually, I looked up at Clive
and saw that he was smiling
rather more broadly
than the situation seemed to call for.
Then he laughed.
Aloud.
A sound
I hadn't heard for months.
Or maybe I hadn't listened.
Anyway, there we were,
crying and laughing
together,
while our mugs of tea and coffee
grew cold.
I feel clean, shriven almost.
I won't say
everything is now coming up roses,
but I will say
we're going to give it a real try here, Clive and I.

He said he needs help with the business,
a thing he's never acknowledged before,
so I can at least do that.
Each week we'll try to go for an excursion –
somewhere we've never been.
He knows I'll still need
a 'fix' of Sydney every now and then.

I also confessed to the encounter with the tree
with my bumper bar,
but Tom Shelley had already told him
when they were working on the church's books.
Small steps, but
a bit of a fresh start nevertheless.
He's not the most exciting man on the planet,
but I'm not the nicest person,
am I?
Clive loves me.
I'm going to try
to return that love.

Beryl Anguis

I made Nance come to the pub with me.
Strength in numbers.
I got Damon out of the way
by forcin' him to do his washin'
so we could sit and drink
and watch and listen.
Didn't take long
for me to work out who was usin' Damon.
Main one was a big bloke,
bald with lots of tatts.
His open collar showed one
that had barbed wire and roses windin' everywhere.
It was even messier 'cause his chest hairs
were all 'tangled' in the wire.
He must of been about forty,
but his sidekick,
copyin' the bald bit with a new-shaved head,
was younger,
twenty-somethin' maybe.
But tough.
Tell you what,
I wouldn't mess with either of them.

They sat in one corner,
and blokes would come,
talk to them in low voices for a coupla minutes
and then leave.
The older one had a grubby-lookin' notebook
and sometimes he'd write a few words in it.
They hardly looked up or around.
Didn't need to.
Some people came to them,

bringing bourbon and beer chasers
as offerings.
So much for me thinkin'
I could go up and ask
what the hell they wanted
with my Damon.
It was creepy
just being in the same pub as them.
Dunno how come Damon
thinks they're okay.
Bet they came on all nice and flatterin',
the cunning bastards.

They didn't stay that long.
Pulled on black beanies
and roared into the dark
on huge Harleys.
As Nance and me left,
I saw that disgusting man
come through the doors
with someone I didn't know.
Couldn't do much about Damon right then,
but why waste an evening?
So I sort of bumped into God-botherer
and said real loud to Nance,
'This is the one
who likes young boys.'

I'd already told her what I seen,
and she'd said, 'You're kiddin' me!'
Real interested, like.
Both Shelley and his mate looked puzzled,

but I swear
preacher man blushed to the roots of his tidy brown hair.
It was loud enough
for people around to hear
and look up from their drinks.
So at least I'd done
somethin' worthwhile with me time.

But what was I gunna do
about those bald thugs
and my boy Damon?

Clive

Tom Shelley rang me
to see if I'd like to go for a drink.
Not really a pub man, myself,
but good of him to ask.
I sensed Ingrid was relieved
to get me out of the house,
doing something with someone else,
a potential friend.
Things have been much better,
but I know she still needs her space.

It was a cool night,
with a sharp blade of frost in the air.
The sky was clear
and hung with stars.
As we walked into the pub,
two women jostled us,
and one of them said something
about liking boys.
No idea what she meant,
or whether she was talking about me or Tom.
He said nothing
but the remark seemed to put him a bit off-balance.

When I told Ingrid later,
she said, 'Well, what did he say about it?'
To her disgust, I hadn't asked.
Didn't seem right.
If Tom didn't want to say,
that's all there was to it.
None of my business.
We talked about other things,

about work,
how our jobs aren't all that different.
Both of us try to make sense of things for people,
things they don't understand,
or want us to understand
for them.
I'm glad I went.
Tom's good company,
We're going to make a weekly thing of it.
Perhaps Ingrid
might like to join us
from time to time.

Tom

The police came to the house today.
Back in Victoria, we had frequent dealings
because my parish was in a big centre.
But here,
I've hardly spoken to them
since I introduced myself back in January.
My parishioners
are not likely to draw the attention of the constabulary,
although I believe Mrs Beattie's a bit of a lead-foot
in that Subaru of hers.

The officer in this case wore his cap,
so I knew no one had died.
But I could tell
he wasn't collecting for the Blue Light Disco either.
I invited him in.
When he did take off his cap,
he spun it nervously around
in knuckly fingers.
His discomfort increased noticeably when he began talking
and I felt sorry for him.
'Um,' he said, 'I just thought
you should be aware,
you should know that
there's been some talk,
only a bit,
but some talk about you
spending time with…um…boys,
young boys.'

At first I had no idea what he was talking about,
and it was a full minute
before the import of his message
hit home.
I was so puzzled at first,
that I didn't think to get angry.
'Boys? What boys?'
What was going on?
Then I remembered.
People describe the sensation of blood running cold.
I now knew what they meant.
Surely not?
Why would she?
The across-street glaring,
the shoving,
the remarks in the pub,
What was the point?
Poison?
'All this and more,' as the books say,
went through my head in that minute.

The only boy I knew,
had had any real dealings with
was Nic Salter.
'Where has this come from?
I asked.

'We can't say at this point,'
the poor guy answered,
seated now,
but still spinning
that damned cap.

'Can you tell us anything
about your meetings
with boys in the church building?'

'Has Nic said anything,
claimed anything?'
'This must be difficult for you,'
was the response.
'I'm sure there's nothing to it,
but I have a duty to make sure everything's above board.'
His embarrassment was genuine,
acute,
so I tried hard not to make him the target
of my anger.
After all, he was just doing his job.
but I felt totally dissociated
from reality.
'It's probably just mischievous gossip at this point,
but you do understand
we need to follow up.'

Mischievous?
I had to sit down myself then,
very heavily.
'You mean malicious, unfounded rubbish, don't you?'
I challenged.
'There is no way,
no way on God's earth,
that I would…'
But couldn't finish the sentence.

'I'm sure it'll all blow over in no time,'
the officer assured me.

'Blow over?'
I knew my voice was rising.
I had to stop repeating what he'd said.
'Do you realise…?'
'Sir, we've kept this case low-profile.
Only on a need-to-know basis.'

'Well, obviously quite a few people
have felt the need to know already,'
I countered.
'This isn't right.'

'I just have to ask you a few questions,'
the miserable man explained.
There followed an interview
about times, places, people,
until I was weary
with the awfulness of it all.
Then a scattering of platitudes,
the offer of a liaison person,
and he left.

I found myself looking out
into the night street,
furtive
as a criminal,
worried
that I'd been seen,
being visited

by a large policeman
in a large police vehicle.
Nothing.
No one.
Except a slight movement
over at Mitch's house,
as the front door closed,
shutting out
the dark.
The V8 was still grumbling away
when the phone rang.

Nic.
'You okay?
The cops were here,
asking about you and me.
I told them to get stuffed.
Who I meet is my business.
Anyway, we're mates.
Gotta go.
Mum wants an explanation.
Talk to you later.
We *are* mates,
aren't we?'

The next morning,
Mr Emmerton called to say
there'd be an extraordinary meeting
of the church council
'to address some concerns that have arisen'.
I was to make myself available
after church on Sunday.

Conducting that service
was one of the hardest things I've ever had to do.
In God's name,
how could I preach to these people,
minister to them,
with this miasma surrounding me?
The meeting was in the church hall
with the thumbtacked notices for playgroup and craft days,
all the chairs piled up,
and the banner proclaiming
'God is Love'
rolled up in the corner.
It was short
and to the point.

I left the gathering bewildered
and very surprised.
All but one present
gave me their total support,
total confidence.

Mrs Beattie tearfully confessed
to telling Emmerton about the Boys Brigade tale.
'I should've known better, Tom.
That mail lady
is no lady at all.'
But then the police had gone to Emmerton anyway,
because in his role as church secretary
'they felt he should be informed'.

Only Mr Wheeler,
who hadn't attended the service earlier,
fronted up for the meeting
and made another display of walking out,
this time muttering,
'Where there's smoke…'

As I walked from that place
in a daze of goodwill,
clean rain began pelting the road,
sweeping dusty leaves and rubbish
into the soon-brimming gutter.
The loveliest moment, though,
was when Mrs Emmerton, who'd been waiting for hubby,
came from their car, patted my hand and said,
'Things will be fine, Tom. You'll see,'
before scurrying back to
the passenger seat
of their immaculate white Holden.

I needed to talk to someone.
So I rang Clive.
Ingrid answered.
Clive was with a client
but would ring straight back.
How was I?
I heard myself telling Ingrid
just how I was.
She listened
without comment.
Then, 'As long as
you don't expect me

to become one of your sheep,
why don't you come
and have dinner with Clive and me?

Mitch

The rain had been comin' down,
right in your face all day.
and wind with it.
The sort of night you just want to stay home
and feel safe.
Didn't feel like working a shift
but I had no choice.
I helped bath the kids
and when I left,
Suzy was tidying up the day's mess.
The whole world seemed unsettled,
angry with itself.
The storm got worse as I drove to the mine.
Had to bend almost double to keep the water
from soaking my face and trickling
under my wet-weather gear.

I went out to the compound
from where I could see the slurry pond.
Not good.
It had happened again.
The water, right up,
spilling over the lip,
trickling down the side
and off into the already-drenched paddocks.
Bloody hell.
It was pissing down
and the thunder grumbled right overhead.
I fumbled for my phone from under
all that clobber
to take photos of what I saw,

and what was scaring me
and making me very angry.
I was just trying to fit the picture
between the diamonds
made by the cyclone wire,
when there was a flash in the sky.
At the same time,
a heavy hand thudded onto my shoulder.
Talk about bein' struck by lightning!
I turned to see the same bloke who'd warned me off last time.
He wasn't happy.
Neither was I.
He'd practically scared the shit out of me,
shoving his face right up against mine
and twisting my arm up behind my back
so that my phone fell onto the squelchy ground.
He stamped on it,
splashing up its own small puddle.
I could hear the crunch
of things breaking.

'Now you listen here, and listen good, Larsen.
I don't think this job
suits scabs like you.
I think we'd better let you go.
Make us all happy.'
I started to protest, but he prodded at me with a gloved fist.
'Don't you worry about the paperwork.
I'll see you get
what's comin' to you.'
He hawked to one side as if to emphasise his point,
his spittle merging with the rain.

'I reckon you should clear out your locker right now,
and have an early mark,
if I were you,
and without any more discussion.'
What did he mean,
'discussion'?
I hadn't said a single word.
But I knew
when I was beat.
I bent to pick up
what was left of my mobile,
but bully boy kicked it
under the wire fence.
I was ropeable.

On the way home
I hardly noticed that the rain was letting up
I was spittin' chips,
but also packin' it.
For one, I'd never told Suzy
about the first time I'd been seen,
and now, I had to go home to her,
earlier than normal,
and jobless.
I was a bit worried
about what they might do to me,
those blokes in charge,
but not as much as I was
nervous about telling my wife.

I was right to be scared.
When Suzy heard the story,
she ripped into me,
yelling and carrying on
so that Cam woke, and stumbled out,
wondering what was going on.
'How could you, Mitch?'
she hammered.
'What are we going to do now?'
I thought she was going to hit me,
she was so cranky,
but after a while
she burned herself out
and slumped into a kitchen chair.
'Sit down, Mitch.'
She still had a top of Carly's in her hands,
and she kept smoothing this out
as she spoke.
'Y'know, I am so pissed off with you,
but also a bit relieved.
I read things, listen,
and I've been getting a bit iffy about you working out there.
But I knew the money was good, and so
I said nothing,
but I'm not real keen on what's happening
to our town and the land around here.'

Suzy had never said a word
about not liking what I did.
I was really surprised,
and sorry
we hadn't talked about it before.

We should've,
but we were both so busy
making sure there was enough.
So here we were, sitting at the kitchen table,
outside, the rain falling,
now more steady and calm.
Cam asleep,
flopped in my arms.
We had some money
from Suze's cleaning job,
and a bit set by.
Surely the mine would pay me some entitlements?
We'd manage.
I wasn't afraid of the future.
I'd do what was needed
to look after my family.

Zoe

It was a brilliant morning,
sharp and clean
after heavy rain over the last few days.
Nic and me were going to show Tom Shelley
around Deep Pools.
When Nic first told me
Mr Shelley would be coming with us,
I was a bit cranky,
even slightly jealous,
because I didn't want to share our special place
with anyone.
But I got over it when I met Mr Shelley.
He was nice.
Not what I expected.
So we got him a bike,
and the three of us pedalled out there,
into the fabulous day.

Nic rode ahead most of the time.
He seemed impatient to get there,
to show Tom
how beautiful Deep Pools was.
I thought I should hang back with Mr Shelley,
because he was as old as Dad
and probably needed to go more slowly.
He was humming to himself as he rode
and didn't make me talk to him.
There were some rough patches
when I realised
he was slowing down
to make sure I was okay!
Maybe he wasn't as unfit as I'd thought.

It's hard telling this now,
but I'll try to remember
just how things happened,
the good and the awful,
because it wasn't all bad.
Although for a while
it seemed so.

Without rushing,
the ride took us about forty minutes.
Nic had gone on ahead
and was already sitting on a rock beside one of the pools,
looking happier
than I'd seen him look for ages.
Almost smug,
as if he'd achieved something important,
completed some sort of quest.
He waved us over.

'Just look at that, eh!
Brilliant, isn't it?'
He could have been holding a banner.
He thought he was King of the Castle.
I loved him then.
So we found rocks that had dried after the rain
and just sat.
Contented.

But Nic couldn't stay still for long.
'Come on, you two, finish your drinks.
I want to show Tom around.'

Tom grinned at me
and gulped down his water.
'Right. Let's go,' he said.
Nic led us up and around
the main pool,
so that we could see right along
where the water had been trapped
into these big ponds
and then escaped through a narrow, steep gorge.
I'd seen it before, of course,
but there was something
in the way Nic showed us that day
that made it different,
fresh again.

He was just like a little kid,
hopping from boulder to boulder,
pointing out
where some rusty mining equipment had been left,
where, if you were careful,
swimming was okay,
and where he and his dad
used to fish.
At one point, I thought I heard
what sounded like a motorbike,
but neither of the others commented
so I forgot about it.

Although the sun shone,
the pools were muddy and swollen after the storms.
I was sorry,

because I wanted it to be perfect
for Nic to show off to Tom.
But he didn't seem to notice.
Here was our tour guide on a real high,
taking us with him.
He was in mid-leap
and mid-sentence,
when we heard what sounded like a deep drum roll,
then a yelp, sliced off by heavy clattering.

Silence,
except for a single crow
shrieking into the hard blue sky.
The racket seemed
to have come from the other side of a small hill.
All three of us rushed over.
Nic got there first.
The slope of the hill had caved in.
A rusty wire gate was hanging open,
and a few metres away
an old red motorbike
lay on the still-damp grass.
The bank was a mess of rubble and mud.
From somewhere in there,
a strangled cry
and the groan of timber settling.

Mr Shelley was first to act.
'Whatever's happened,
we'll need an ambulance.
Zoe, take your bike and ride until you get reception,
and then ring.'

Tom

I sent Zoe for help
so that Nic and I could get digging.
Someone was under this mess,
and the quicker we were,
the better our chances.
Nic was amazing.
Before Zoe had pedalled away,
he'd dragged over a couple of fallen branches
for us to dig with.

We set to,
hurling mud, dirt, grass
out of the way,
sometimes shoving the branches aside
to dig in the dirt with bare hands.
From time to time,
we could hear moaning
and what sounded like some pretty lurid swearing.
Someone was there,
alive and in pain.

There was no talk between Nic and me,
just grunting and a bit of our own swearing.
The last obstacles
we came to were rotted beams,
splintery,
but still heavy.
Nic and I heaved
together,
and finally managed
to haul them out of the way.
Now we could see more clearly:

Legs trapped under more timber
and the top half of someone
covered by rubble.
One arm was free,
trying to shift stuff away from a face,
but stones kept trickling back.
Nic jumped down
and, like a terrier, scrabbled away
until he'd cleared enough rocks to see a face.

'Holy shit!' I heard him exclaim.
And he leaned back against the side of the hole
to catch his breath.
'Damon bloody Anguis!'

Damon's response was a muffled whine.

'Come on, Nic, keep at it,' I urged.
'Still have to get him out,
whoever he is.'

Nic shook his head
as if he'd come out of hypnosis,
knelt wordlessly
and carefully lifted the rest of the stones
from Damon's face.
Then I got down into the hole we'd made.
It was a tight squeeze
but it was best if we didn't try to move him.

Then Nic bent to Damon.
'You'll be right, mate. Just hang in there.'
The two of us

shouldered away the final beams,
and they bounced
onto the rest of the debris.
In the cavity beside Damon
there were several hessian sacks,
bulging and lumpy, as if they carried young joeys.
By the time we'd managed to heave them out,
I had a pretty good idea of their contents
and opened the neck of one sack
to have my suspicions confirmed.
We didn't have time to open each one
and didn't need to.

Nic's hands were filthy
and bleeding like mine,
our faces smeared with soil and sweat.
We looked at each other
and made time for a smile,
before checking the damage to Damon's legs.

His response to our request
to see if he could move either leg,
was, 'I'm fucked. Can't shift a thing.
Just get me out, willya?'
I nearly laughed,
and it was Nic who said,
'Mate, the ambulance will be here soon.
Just hang on if you can. I'll fetch you a drink.'
He hauled himself up and went to get water.
Damon grabbed the bottle
with his good hand, gulped down most of it,

and poured the rest
over the mess of his face,
wincing with the pain.

Nic must have been thirsty himself by then,
but he said nothing.
I'd drunk all my water earlier.
I did think to get my jumper
and put it so that Damon's face was shaded.
But there was no doubt
who was in control here –
a young man called Nic Salter.
We'd just sat back on our haunches,
sweaty and mud-streaked
when in the distance
two sirens, their wailing filling the air.

Unbidden, those lines came to mind –
'I sprang to the stirrup,
I galloped, Dirk galloped…' –
and although it was hardly good news she'd carried,
I thought of the effort
Zoe must have put into her riding.
Some girl, that.

Nic

Once the ambulance was there,
I kind of conked out,
because we'd been digging pretty hard.
I looked for Zoe,
in case she'd come back with the ambos.
Instead, Damon's mum was there,
carrying on a treat.
Don't think she could decide
whether to swear at her son
or cry a lot because he'd been hurt.
So she did both, making heaps of noise,
looking over at Tom and me,
as if we were somehow to blame
for the whole thing.

Trust that Damon Anguis
to be up to something dodgy.
Tom and the policeman
moved the sacks over to the side.
I could hear them talking quietly
as they undid the ties
and peered at the stuff.
But I couldn't be bothered moving,
so just let things happen around me.
The ambos were fantastic and
did their thing so smoothly.

Tom came back over and plonked himself down
just as a medic spoke to us.
'You look done in, you two.
Let's check you out.'
He cleaned us up real well,

and I felt quite important sitting there,
hands cleanly bandaged.
Tom had a deep cut on his arm,
probably from a nail or splinter.
He got to have a sling.
We sat, like a couple of wounded soldiers,
grinning at each other.
We'd done good,
and I felt terrific.
They couldn't fit both of us in the ambulance,
but a council truck was on its way
to shore up and cordon off
the damage.

With a knowing smile,
Tom said I should go to check on Zoe.
He'd be happy to wait
and just relax for a while.
So off I went, dirty,
sweaty, blood-smudged,
but more contented somehow
than I'd been
for months.

Tom

Nic went back to town
in the front of the ambulance.
It rocked its way across the paddocks,
siren keening.
I think he fancied himself
a bit of a hero.
And he was.

The police officer
walked around the site,
making notes and taking photos.
He said, 'You've had a pretty torrid time lately, haven't you?'
I nodded, but you know,
I didn't feel as battle-weary
as I might have.

When the officer left,
the quiet was so complete
I could hear myself breathe.
It was just marvellous.
They'd left me some water,
so I just sat
and listened to the earth.
My mind was full,
and my middle-aged body was beginning to ache,
but it was good here.
I could see
why Nic and his dad
had found it so special.

I'd hardly moved
when I heard the council truck.

It came bouncing towards
me, carrying four men.
These blokes really got on with it.
They had plenty of tools
and knew what they were doing.
So I wandered off on my own
towards the water.
It certainly looked deep and murky,
almost sinister,
but I could imagine a day
when it would be clear and blue
and inviting.

Then a shout and an oath from the cave-in site.
I saw one man drop his shovel
and stumble away to throw up
in the grass.
He was followed by another,
while the remaining two
looked down towards the dropped tools.
No more shouting,
but a lot more cursing and gagging.
I went towards them
but was warned off. 'No mate, just stay.
Stay there.'

His offsider said,
'It's the new minister, Ken. He'll be right.'
I recognised Mrs Beattie's son.
They moved aside to let me see.
I wish they hadn't.
Further along the exposed shaft,

behind another tumble
of collapsed rock and timber,
I recognised what was left
of a body –
a skeleton tented
by leathery skin,
propped against the wall of the shaft,
knees up under a grimacing skull,
mouth open in a silent scream.
Beyond this grotesque travesty of a human,
lay something else.
A fishing rod.
Snapped roughly
into three pieces.

Mitch

In the *Tillers Gap Tele* they had a front-page article
about what happened out at Deep Pools.
I felt really bad
having avoided Tom for weeks.
I was a bit cranky that he hadn't
done anything about the mine.
Not that I had either. Just got myself sacked.
I guess I felt bad about the time Suzy had said
there was no one home, but I'll admit her finding that jumper
did get to me a bit.
And then there were these rumours,
stuff about Tom and young boys.
If I'd been embarrassed to be seen
with a church person before, I sure didn't want
to hang around with one, especially Tom Shelley,
not after that.

Now I'm sorry,
and angry with myself.
It's time I made up my own mind about things.
And people.
I'd lost my job and felt like shit.
I hadn't realised what a big part of my life
going to work had been.
Suze found out about a TAFE course
for a diesel mechanic.
I've started that.
Have to drive to Katoomba for classes,
so used that as an excuse
not to go and see how Tom is.
Now there's all this in the paper,
about him and Nic Salter and Damon Anguis.

Made it clear
that Tom Shelley was a bit of a hero.
Told myself to get over there and apologise.
But Tom Shelley came to me.
Suzy was out with both kids,
so we had the time and the quiet to talk.
I started to tell him,
but he stopped me.

'I just wanted to pop over for a jif,' he said.
'See how you're travelling.' I told him
about work, about TAFE, and tried again
to say sorry.
No luck this time, either.
It was as if we'd been to the pub
the week before.
I admitted that things were a bit tight
and Tom offered his support. He said
he knew a good bloke, an accountant
who, he was sure, would help us
get things organised and under control.
Tom would help with fees, but he doubted
this man would want much.
I hadn't thought of getting an accountant in.
I mean, we'd always just managed.
Accountants were for other people.
But I could see that it was a really good idea.

Then Tom said,
'Actually, I wanted to ask Suzy something.
Do you think she'd come and help
with the catering for a lunch
after Nic's dad's funeral?

We're a bit short-handed.
I think there might be quite a crowd,
and some of the older church ladies
can get a bit flustered.
Someone young would be great.'

Would you believe Clive Pallister was the man Tom had in mind?
So we went, Suzy and me, to see him.
He was great.
He helped us feel that we could get things back on track,
and said he'd be happy to continue the relationship.
Who'd have thought Suzy and I would ever say
'Our accountant?'
Sounds pretty good to me.

Suzy was really glad to help after the funeral.
She felt as bad as me,
and wanted to do something
to make up for what she'd been thinking.

Beryl Anguis

Can't believe I wanted to know
what Damon was doing all day.
He's driving me up the wall.
Lyin' there, his leg in plaster that's already filthy, with dirt
and disgusting comments from his mates.
Crutch propped up against the lounge,
the TV on all bloody day:
The People's Court, re-runs of *Jag*.
He doesn't care what's showin'.
The only time he perks up is when
his mates come round.
Then they all sit there, with the TV still on,
eatin' me out of house and home.
I've had it with these kids, I'm tellin ya.

'Any more coke in the frig, Mrs A?'
one of them asked.
It was the last time he did.

'Can't see that your leg's broken, Tim Keesing.
Get your own bloody drinks. Better still,
bring your own, you lazy bugger.'

Tim just laughed, but after they'd gone
Damon told me not to talk to his mates like that.
It was another last time.
'Listen, my boy,' I said, 'I'm sick and bloody tired
of waitin' on you hand and foot. I'm not gunna do it
for your useless friends as well.'

Because Damon hadn't turned eighteen,
his little problem with the law was kept out of the courts.

Last year,
when he was supposed to have stolen equipment from school,
he got a caution.
This time,
we had to go to a thing called a Youth Conference.
There was a big table we had to sit around,
while the 'matter was dealt with'.
Damon was shit-scared.
Seein' him like that, I could see
he was a coward, just like his old man.
It was 'Yes, sir. No, sir. Three bags full, sir' with him.
Wuss.
Lots of times I tried to tell 'em he was the victim here,
he'd never been given a fair go.
They ought to look around a bit, open their eyes.
but my boy Damon was only too happy to cooperate.
Told them the whole story,
gave them names, dates, places,
only too keen to spill his guts.
Described the blokes in the pub.
Not as well as I could, mind,
but they wouldn't let me get a word in.
Had to keep interruptin'.
In the end one of the coppers,
some butch-lookin' chick with spiky blonde hair
warned me that I'd have to wait outside
if I didn't stop interferin' with the proceedings.
Bitch.

And now I've ended up
with my layabout of a son hanging around the house all day.
Now that there's no money comin' in,

he bludges off me all the time
for rubbish like lollies, fizzy drink, hamburgers, chips.
Just like a little kid. A real slob of a kid.
He's not allowed near the pub now, of course.
Wish he was. He's nothin' but a pain in the backside here.
With his just-as-useless mates
droppin' round after school. They all just sit there,
sloped into the furniture, and talk in grunts,
with the odd bark of laughter.
Not happy, Damon.

Jim Salter got a real send-off.
I just happened to be doing my rounds
near the church at the time.
Big do, it was. Don't know if you'd call it a funeral,
but whatever it was,
you could hear the singin'
way up the street.
I just sat on me bike and listened for a while,
the music comin' at me through the drizzle.

Ingrid

On the day of Jim Salter's funeral
it rained again, but lightly, gently,
as if in benediction.
There was a wonderful turnout
and lots of celebrating life
rather than mourning.
Nic spoke about his dad,
all the things Jim had taught him,
how he knew his father
would never have abandoned him and his mum.
Mr Salter would have been so proud.
I know Nic's mum was. Teary,
but proud.

Tom asked me if I'd help
prepare and serve luncheon after the service.
Some of the quilting ladies were there, too.
so was Suzy Larsen.
It was fun working with these women
and, once again,
I was glad to be part of something.
From our place in the hall,
we could hear the singing.
I ducked out and stood near the door
so I could listen to the eulogies.
Then Tom's voice,
steady and clear.

After the service, Nic came into the hall,
looking so grown up
so certain of his place.
He made sure his mum wasn't alone,

but also let Zoe fuss over him.
The police were able to piece together what had happened.
Mr Salter had gone fishing,
but must have heard a vehicle
and seen men unloading the stolen gear
and stashing it in the abandoned shaft.
Jim Salter confronted the men,
who took to him with a rusty length of something
left there after the mine closed.
There was a scuffle,
leaving one man dead and
two men guilty and secretive.
Damon hadn't known about the body
being there, had only
hidden things in the shaft
over the last few months.
Apparently, he had nearly fallen over himself
to 'assist police with their enquiries'.

Over dinner at our place,
Tom had told us about Nic and the hassles he'd had.
I had a feeling that very few empty-headed bullies
would bother Nic Salter from now on.
After everyone had gone, it took a while
to get everything cleaned up and tidy.
I was tired from all the standing,
but I'd actually enjoyed myself.
Zoe had stayed to help, and was sweeping the floor.
Tom had taken Nic's mum home
while Nic, Mitch and Clive dismantled
trestle tables and put chairs away.
Bundling up the wet tea towels to take home,

I looked around me.
Here we were.
An unlikely crew, almost friends,
working together, laughing.
As we left the church,
the sun burst through the clouds.
Tomorrow would be fine.

www.ingramcontent.com/pod-product-compliance
Lightning Source LLC
Chambersburg PA
CBHW070900080526
44589CB00013B/1147